PHILOSOPHY OF PSYCHOLOGY

PRENTICE-HALL FOUNDATIONS OF PHILOSOPHY SERIES

Virgil Aldrich	Philosophy of Art
William Alston	Philosophy of Language
Roderick M. Chisholm	Theory of Knowledge 2E
Lawrence H. Davis	Theory of Action
William Dray	Philosophy of History
C. Dyke	Philosophy of Economics
Joel Feinberg	Social Philosophy
William K. Frankena	Ethics 2E
Martin P. Golding	Philosophy of Law
Carl Hempel	Philosophy of Natural Science
John Hick	Philosophy of Religion 3E
David L. Hull	Philosophy of Biological Science
James E. McClellan	Philosophy of Education
Joseph Margolis	Philosophy of Psychology
Willard Van Orman Quine	Philosophy of Logic
Richard Rudner	Philosophy of Social Science
Wesley C. Salmon	Logic 3E
Jerome Shaffer	Philosophy of Mind
Richard Taylor	Metaphysics 3E

Elizabeth Beardsley, Monroe Beardsley,
and Tom L. Beauchamp, editors

PHILOSOPHY OF PSYCHOLOGY

Joseph Margolis
Temple University

PRENTICE-HALL, INC., Englewood Cliffs, New Jersey 07632

Library of Congress Cataloging in Publication Data

MARGOLIS, JOSEPH ZALMAN (date)
Philosophy of psychology.

(Prentice-Hall foundations of philosophy series)
Bibliography.
Includes index.
1. Psychology—Philosophy. I. Title. II. Series.
BF38.M37 1984 150′.1 83-13958
ISBN 0–13–664326–4

Editorial/production supervision: F. Hubert
Manufacturing buyer: Harry P. Baisley

Printed in the United States of America

10 9 8 7 6 5 4 3 2 1

ISBN 0-13-664326-4

PRENTICE-HALL INTERNATIONAL, INC., *London*
PRENTICE-HALL OF AUSTRALIA PTY. LIMITED, *Sydney*
EDITORA PRENTICE-HALL DO BRASIL, LTDA., *Rio de Janeiro*
PRENTICE-HALL CANADA INC., *Toronto*
PRENTICE-HALL OF INDIA PRIVATE LIMITED, *New Delhi*
PRENTICE-HALL OF JAPAN, INC., *Tokyo*
PRENTICE-HALL OF SOUTHEAST ASIA PTE. LTD., *Singapore*
WHITEHALL BOOKS LIMITED, *Wellington, New Zealand*

for Monroe Beardsley
with the warmest wishes

Contents

Foundations of Philosophy

Many of the problems of philosophy are of such broad relevance to human concerns, and so complex in their ramifications, that they are, in one form or another, perennially present. Though in the course of time they yield in part to philosophical inquiry, they may need to be rethought by each age in the light of its broader scientific knowledge and deepened ethical and religious experience. Better solutions are found by more refined and rigorous methods. Thus, one who approaches the study of philosophy in the hope of understanding the best of what it affords will look for both fundamental issues and contemporary achievements.

Written by a group of distinguished philosophers, the Foundations of Philosophy Series aims to exhibit some of the main problems in the various fields of philosophy as they stand at the present stage of philosophical history.

While certain fields are likely to be represented in most introductory courses in philosophy, college classes differ widely in emphasis, in method of instruction, and in rate of progress. Every instructor needs freedom to change his course as his own philosophical interests, the size and makeup of his classes, and the needs of his students vary from year to year. The nineteen volumes in the Foundations of Philosophy Series—each complete in itself, but complementing the others—offer a new flexibility to the instructor, who can create his own textbook by combining several volumes as he wishes, and can choose different combinations at different times. Those volumes that are not used in an introductory course will be found valuable, along with other texts or collections or readings, for the more specialized upper-level courses.

Elizabeth Beardsley / *Monroe Beardsley* / *Tom L. Beauchamp*
Temple University   Temple University   Georgetown University

Preface

I find myself returning constantly to two nagging reflections: first, the technical one that psychology cannot possibly be an autonomous science; second, the humane one that we cannot possibly hope to capture our own nature by any totalizing formula. On review, I see that I have somehow managed to weave both reflections into the fabric of my account of the principal theories of psychological theory. I must confess that I find that outcome reassuring, though I have not the slightest sense of having forced the account in these respects. On the contrary, these reflections seem to have emerged as rather powerful meta-theories of their own, pointing the way to a balanced appraisal of the strength and limitation of the leading types of theories. A major puzzle about psychology has always been whether it most resembles physics or literature. I suggest in the pages that follow that it resembles both and that, consequently, it both enlarges our conception of what it is to be a science and confirms its systematic continuity with certain of the humanities.

Although the two reflections mentioned may reasonably be said to guide my account, I have tried to make the gauge of this report finer than such airy remarks would seem to promise; and I have tried to draw the discussion of the important theories entirely from the actual remarks of their principal advocates. I hope I have caught the flavor and substance of the essential debates. In this sense, I should like the discussion to appear as a sort of dialogue of how we have theorized—chiefly in the twentieth century—about how we should best theorize about the human mind (and by extension, the minds of animals). Quite remarkably, the historical shifts among the principal sorts of theories show an orderly progression from one to another that matches very neatly the conceptual stages of a unified and systematic analysis. There is more than an impression of inevitability with which one movement has replaced another. But that, precisely, is what I have tried to capture. It is the only way I know of assisting others to gain a genuinely effective grip on a tradition or practice of inquiry, so that they, too, may contribute to it—even if at the expense of superceding their own instructors.

I have benefited from comments on earlier, rather unwieldy, versions of the manuscript: particularly those of Monroe Beardsley, Hugh Lacey, and Robert Matthews, whom I count as friends, and of an anonymous reader for Prentice-Hall who performed his or her duties in a most helpful way; also from regular discussions about the empirical issues of psychology as well, with Charles Reed and Robert Weisberg; and from late discussions, in person and by letter, with Michael Krausz, Donald Callen, and Tom Beauchamp. The typing of the finished manuscript I owe, as so often before, entirely to Grace Stuart; there's a debt there that I won't even try to discharge.

J.M.

PHILOSOPHY OF PSYCHOLOGY

CHAPTER ONE

Orientation

In all the disciplines concerned with the analysis and explanation of psychological phenomena, there is at least one clear theme that yields a strong sense of an overview gradually developing in an orderly and manageable way through very large theoretical claims. The story of that theme is rather pretty, because there is a certain instructive inevitability in moving from one stage of these theories to another. One cannot fail to be struck by the impression that the inquiries in question seem to have arranged themselves in a more or less historical succession that corresponds to the stages of a rational and single-minded debate.

The movement of this somewhat idealized argument may be taken to fix what we shall here call *philosophy of psychology*. There is no such course of study that is well known by that name. What, in the Anglo-American tradition, has been called "philosophy of mind" or "philosophical psychology" has been largely occupied with exorcising—down to our own day—the influence of so-called *Cartesian dualism,* the classical source of which lies in the work of the seventeenth-century philosopher, René Descartes. It may seem extraordinary that Descartes's influence should have been so vital that even relatively recent contributions in the philosophy of mind remain somewhat preoccupied with his concerns. But it is fair to say that within British and American philosophy of the last forty years, many of the most influential and respected contributions—notably, Gilbert Ryle's *The Concept of Mind* (1949) and Herbert Feigl's *The "Mental" and the "Physical"* (1958/1967)—are explicitly focused on one or another of Descartes's doctrines. Effectively, this has meant that philosophical speculation has, until quite recently, tended to pay rather little attention to the detailed studies of the relevant empirical sciences or to the conceptual issues those sciences have raised in their own specialized ways. Correspondingly, the philosophy of mind has tended to discuss only in the most cursory way (if at all) the rich biological, cultural, historical, perceptual, affective, even linguistic features of actual human existence. These have almost always been construed as providing an extremely bland and sketchy background for a variety of conventional topics loosely connected with one another within the philosophical tradition.

The usual abstract questions explored in the philosophy of mind have included the following:

whether there are important differences between the numerical identity of persons and physical bodies;
whether inner mental states are ascribable at all;
whether a completely private language is possible;
whether psychophysical causal interaction can be denied on conceptual grounds;
the nature of choice or free action;
the difference between reasons and causes;
whether the admission of psychological causes is compatible with determinism;
the essential mark of mental properties;
whether we have indubitable knowledge of our own mental states;
whether the mind (or its "contents"—thoughts, pains, and the like) is a distinct entity;
what is meant by intentionality;
what conceptual difficulties confront the construing of mental phenomena as purely physical phenomena.

These have been the standard topics (see Shaffer, 1968). However, both from the side of philosophy and from the side of the relevant empirical disciplines, emphasis has now begun to shift to such issues as these:

the difference between the cognitive abilities of human persons and animals;
the prospects of artificial intelligence and of the machine simulation of intelligence;
the maturation and developmental processes of humans;
the analysis of linguistic ability in biological and psychological terms;
the psychophysical processes of thought, perception, memory, abstraction, learning, and the like;
the complexity of the cultural and historical conditions of human existence;
the relationship between individual persons and the societies in which they are groomed and function.

As a result, the newer philosophical currents are distinctly closer to scientific concerns, that is, distinctly more systematic and better informed empirically. In fact, the demarcation between a purely philosophical overview of the conceptual issues and the theoretical speculations of the empirical disciplines involved has become increasingly difficult (and increasingly unnecessary) to draw.

The focus of this newer convergence between philosophy and psychology is a natural one: the provision of a conceptual framework within which the explanation of human sentience and intelligence may be adequately organized. This is the unifying theme mentioned earlier, the theme of the somewhat newly minted discipline of philosophy of psychology. It may not seem to mark much of a departure from the classic concerns of the philosophy of mind; and, indeed, there is bound to be overlap between the two. But what is distinctive about the new convergence is that philosophical inquiries are now pointedly addressed to drawing their questions out of the detailed studies of the pertinent empirical disciplines—biology, neurophysiology, psychology, psychophysics, ethology, linguistics, information science, sociology, anthropology, medicine, psychoanalysis, history, even literary and art criticism. At the same time, psychology has gradually rediscovered the central importance of an adequate theoretical understanding of the nature of human cognition. All the pertinent disciplines now see their converging interests in fashioning a conceptual schema within which the entire range of detailed questions about the cognitive work and accomplishments of humans can be productively integrated. Thus, the narrative thread of the various theoretical movements we shall examine is much like a systematic argument gradually unfolding through an extended interval of time.

The principal source of tension and dispute in this story is undoubtedly due to the double attraction of trying to construe the science of psychology as falling comfortably within the scope of the investigative methods and explanatory procedures of the physical sciences and of trying to enlarge the conception of an empirical science in order to accommodate those features of psychological inquiry that seem incapable of being thus characterized. This is still the principal source of tension and dispute within the context of the philosophy of psychology. It has been complicated further by the relatively recent appearance of a large literature in the history of science and the history of the philosophy of science that has quite fundamentally challenged the most standard views of the norms and paradigms of empirical inquiry, explanation, confirmation, causal laws, and the like in physics and astronomy (see, for instance, Feyerabend, 1975; Kuhn, 1962/1970; Lakatos, 1978). It now seems as if the physical sciences have prospered without actually conforming to the explanatory and confirmatory models they were thought to favor—perhaps, most notably, for our present purpose, the model advanced by the so-called unity of science program, which we shall consider in due course (see Carnap, 1932–33/1959, 1931/1934; Causey, 1977; Neurath, 1938). If that were true there could be little reason to treat psychology as scientifically dubious or deviant if it failed to conform to such models; if, in addition, psychological phenomena resist analysis solely in physical terms, there could be little reason to deny psychology scientific status merely because its methods of inquiry and explanation were not identical with those of physics.

The narrative of the argument begins, then, with the principal conceptual strategies by which psychological phenomena are treated as completely congruent with the leading features of the physical sciences. Increasingly, these have appeared unpromising and unconvincing. More recent theories have conceded that psychological phenomena are distinct from the purely physical. Understandably, they have done so in the most conservative way possible—resisting, on the one hand, any return to Cartesian dualism and promoting, on the other, the least alteration in the conception of what a science is.

If we confined ourselves, say, to the past half century, we could readily classify the principal, most actively debated, most promising theories within the scope of the philosophy of psychology—within both professional psychology and professional philosophy—as being of one or another of the following four varieties: *reductive materialism, behaviorism, functionalism,* and *cognitivism.* The two tendencies regarding the relation between psychology and physics divide quite nicely between the first and second pairs of the theories just mentioned.

If so, we are the beneficiaries of a very convenient economy. It would be utterly hopeless to attempt to survey the sprawling research of psychology with an eye to drawing orderly conclusions about such issues as learning, perception, affect, sexual development, acquisition of language, pattern recognition, cultural imprinting, and the like. Nevertheless, it is entirely fair to suppose that much of importance in psychology cannot be entirely subsumed under the options favored by the four general movements just mentioned. For example, Jean Piaget's so-called genetic structuralism (1968/1970) cannot be easily construed as a variation of any of these movements. Nevertheless, the distinction of Piaget's theory becomes particularly legible in the context of exploring what we are here calling cognitivism (see, for example, Piattelli-Palmarini, 1980). It is to be hoped that a similar relationship can be established for most of the important general psychological theories. Freudian metapsychology, for example, seems to have distinct affinities with all of the four movements mentioned.

We shall examine, then, these four sorts of theories, with a view not so much to the history of psychology as to the potential adequacy of any conceptual orientation regarding the phenomena of cognition. Here, the principal concerns on which nearly all discussants converge surely include at least the following:

1. the avoidance of Cartesian dualism, which is thought to be inimical to empirical science, however generously construed;
2. dialectical tensions regarding the adequacy of such models of science as that advanced by the unity of science program;
3. the relative autonomy of psychology as a science, particularly with respect to social and cultural processes pertinent to the explanation of psychological phenomena.

The last of these issues we shall only touch on briefly, not because it is unimportant, but rather because it bears on the limitations of all four movements to be examined. It invites us to consider quite heterodox possibilities far beyond a survey of the prevailing currents of philosophy of psychology (more or less centered in the Anglo-American literature). In fact, it would invite a serious review of the relationship between the Anglo-American and a large Continental literature that included contributions from phenomenology, hermeneutics, Marxism, structuralism, semiotics, and related movements. Clearly, this would require an entirely new undertaking—which, it must be said, is already incipient in recent efforts.

It would be useful to fix a little more explicitly the thrust of Cartesian dualism, on which the branching of the philosophy of mind and philosophy of psychology so much depends. Two sample remarks may serve us here. The first is taken from Ryle's *The Concept of Mind* (1949), probably the first of the most influential accounts of mind in the Anglo-American philosophical literature of the last fifty years. It shows very clearly Ryle's own anti-Cartesian bent and something of the stubborn vigor of Descartes's dualism down to our own day. One of the central motives of his book, Ryle (1949) says:

> . . . is to show that "mental" does not denote a status, such that one can sensibly ask of a given thing or event whether it is mental or physical, "in the mind" or "in the outside world." To talk of a person's mind is not to talk of a repository which is permitted to house objects that something called "the physical world" is forbidden to house; it is to talk of the person's abilities, liabilities and inclinations to do and undergo certain sorts of things, and of the doing and undergoing of these things in the ordinary world (p. 199).

Ryle's statement is rather curious. Although he obviously wishes to resist the notion of two distinct "worlds"—an "inner" (mental) and an "outer" (physical) world (the thesis of Cartesian dualism)—he concedes the usefulness of the distinction of the mental, provided it remains restricted to sorting "abilities, liabilities and inclinations." But he is so much preoccupied with avoiding the dangers of Cartesian thinking that he instinctively slights such puzzling phenomena as those of feeling or being aware of pain, which threaten to reinstate (Ryle fears) "inner objects" (pains).

Notoriously, Descartes included in his account of a "thinking thing" (mind) such attributes as the capacity to *doubt* (or believe) and to *feel* (pain and other sensations), without suitably distinguishing between the two: "What is a thing which thinks? [he asks.] It is a thing which doubts, understands, conceives, affirms, denies, wills, refuses, which also imagines and feels" (*Meditations,* II; Haldane & Ross, 1911–12/1934; see Geach, 1957; Vendler, 1972). So, for Descartes, there is a sense in which feeling pain is a form of thinking. (He is uneasy about this, because he thinks animals feel pain while lacking minds.) The usual reason advanced for Descartes's questionable maneuver is that he supposed there was an "essence" or uniform nature ("thinking") to all phenomena properly called mental that distinguished them utterly from the physical. This is the source of so-called *Cartesian dualism.* In the nineteenth century, Franz Brentano (1874/1973) attempted in the Cartesian spirit to specify once and for all what *essentially* distinguished mind and body, recovering the medieval notion of *intentionality* as the "mark" of the mental—suited more, so it seemed (to Brentano and many others) to doubting and believing than to pain and sensations of warmth. (The important topic of intentionality will occupy us throughout our account.)

The second remark comes from a recent book of Richard Rorty (1979). It confirms, precisely in disputing the adequacy of Brentano's solution to the Cartesian problem, the surprising persistence of the search for what is essential to the mental:

> The obvious objection to defining the mental as the intentional is that pains are not intentional—they do not represent, they are not about anything. The obvious objection to defining the mental as "the phenomenal" is that beliefs don't feel like anything—they don't have phenomenal properties, and a person's real beliefs are not always what they appear to be. The attempt to hitch pains and beliefs together seems ad hoc—they don't seem to have anything in common except our refusal to call them "physical" (p. 22).

Here, the point of connection and disconnection between traditional inquiries in the philosophy of mind and the new concerns of philosophy of psychology make themselves felt. For without insisting on any form of essentialism, certainly without advocating Cartesian dualism, what most naturally distinguishes the mental or psychological is just the *ability of organisms (or systems) to have and acquire cognitive states,* the ability to believe or know or feel or be aware of something, to desire or intend or plan or fear—which entails an ability to believe and know. Here is the simple, obvious linkage between what critics of Descartes have segregated as the "phenomenal" and "intentional" aspects of mental life.

The bearing of the puzzles of Cartesian dualism on the puzzles of dialectical tensions is quite direct, for both the "phenomenal" and the "intentional" features of mental life raise fundamental questions about psychology as a science. This is straightforwardly clear from two other influential remarks that deserve consideration. The first is by J. J. C. Smart (1963), who infers much about the ultimate nature of the mental *from* an antecedent appeal to the explanatory power of the physical sciences:

> It looks today as though the ultimate laws of nature are those of physics. . . . Now, if there are *qualia* [perceived, phenomenal qualities, like the redness of a tomato], then they cannot plausibly be fitted into this sort of scheme. . . . Human psychology cannot be entirely fitted into a physicalist science. There would have to be special irreducible laws . . . (p. 68).

Smart finds such irreducible laws "hard to believe in" because they seem so "uncharacteristic of the general development of our scientific knowledge." Clearly, he has reversed the usual order of inquiry.

In somewhat the same spirit, W. V. Quine (1960), who has developed one of the dominant philosophical accounts of the last twenty-five years, rejects intentional phenomena:

> One may accept the Brentano thesis [regarding the analysis of the mental in terms of intentionality] either as showing the indispensability of intentional idioms and the importance of an autonomous science of intention, or as showing the baselessness of intentional idioms and the emptiness of a science of intention. My attitude, unlike Brentano's, is the second. To accept intentional usage at face value is . . . to postulate translation relations as somehow objectively valid though indeterminate in principle relative to the totality of speech dispositions. Such postulation promises little gain in scientific insight if there is no better ground for it than that the supposed translation relations are presupposed by the vernacular of semantics and intention (p. 221).

Smart rejects phenomenal *qualia* because they fail to suit the system of natural laws the physical sciences have compellingly supplied. Quine rejects intentional phenomena because the idiom required to characterize them fails to conform with the kind of rigor now favored in the scientific enterprise. In much the same spirit (as we shall see), B. F. Skinner rejects explanation in mental terms altogether. But *if* we cannot otherwise justifiably replace or discard the phenomenal and the intentional—or eliminate the mental altogether—these are dubious maneuvers. The admission of psychology as a science, therefore, may ultimately entail a considerable revision in our notion of what a science is.

CHAPTER TWO

Reductionism

SETTING THE PROBLEM

Put in the baldest way, all systematic efforts to describe, identify, and explain the phenomena of sentience and intelligence and the nature of the organisms and systems that exhibit sentience and intelligence are focused on two issues: (1) whether such phenomena and such entities are purely physical in nature; (2) whether, in the context of scientific explanation, it is possible to account for such phenomena in terms adequate for explanation in the fundamental physical sciences. Are human persons, for example, simply complex physical bodies? Can playing a chess game be explained in terms akin to those judged adequate for explaining the behavior of colliding billiard balls or the chemistry of the blood? Affirmative views are said to be *reductive* or reductionistic: *ontologically,* with respect to the first issue; *methodologically,* with respect to the second.

These are relatively independent issues. For instance, it is entirely possible that although human persons are actually nothing but physical bodies possessing nothing but physical properties (so-called *physicalism*) (see Nagel, 1965), there are conceptual or practical difficulties confronting any serious attempt to replace completely a psychological idiom with a physical one (see Davidson, 1970; Fodor, 1975; Putnam, 1978). Perhaps humans *are* complex automata. Even so, it is improbable that, say, the activities of marriage counseling or real estate speculation would be fundamentally affected by the demonstration that they are. It is improbable unless, as Richard Rorty

(1979) confidently supposes, "Every speech, thought, theory, poem, composition, and philosophy will turn out to be completely predictable in purely naturalistic terms. . . . [Within the terms of] some atoms-and-the void account of micro-processes within individual human beings . . . there are no ghosts" (p. 387). On the other hand, it may be that within the explanatory concerns of genuine science (however construed), an idiom restricted to purely physical distinctions will prove to be adequate for psychology, with or without a resolution of the first issue (see Brodbeck, 1966; Feigl, 1958/1967; Körner, 1966; J. B. Watson, 1925).

The union of ontological and methodological reduction was most explicitly and fully advocated in the so-called unity of science movement (see Causey, 1977; Neurath, 1938; Oppenheim & Putnam, 1958), although, for reasons associated with the history of positivism, the expression *ontological reduction* was not characteristically favored. In effect, the *unity of science* held physics to be the paradigm of a genuine science, in the sense, broadly speaking, that: (1) its investigative and explanatory canons were taken to be normative for all sciences, and (2) the range of terms or predicates sufficient for its descriptive and explanatory work were taken to be, in principle, sufficient for all would-be sciences as well. Herbert Feigl's formulation of this dual objective is probably the most familiar short version cited (see Meehl & Sellars, 1956). By "physical," Feigl (1958/1967) says he means "the [general] type of concepts and laws which suffice in principle for the explanation and prediction of inorganic processes"; and by "physical$_2$" (which captures the reductive intent of both aspects of the unity of science program), he means the extension and application of what falls under the "physical" to "the phenomena of organic life" (including sentience and more developed psychological phenomena) (p. 10).

Feigl himself is entirely candid about the difficulty of the reductive program; in fact, he incorporates it in the most explicit way into his own formulation. For instance, he concedes the impossibility of separating the achievement of a fully reductive science from that of being able to provide a similarly reductive account of the work of the very scientists who contribute to physics. Here, he introduces the special notion of "physical$_1$," that is, the property of "a conceptual system anchored in sensory observation and designed for increasingly comprehensive and coherent explanations of the intersubjectively confirmable facts of observation." The scope of the physical sciences, then, depends on the ability to explain the very production of those sciences—of physical$_1$ phenomena—in physical$_2$ terms. In short, however we may adjust the objectives of ontological and methodological reduction, we cannot plausibly ignore the puzzle of how to explain in suitably scientific terms *the phenomenon of human science itself*. This suggests a much closer conceptual connection between the two issues than some theorists would press; and it confirms the conceptual linkage between the explanatory efforts of the strictest sciences with those regarding ordinary psychological, social, and cultural phenomena (see Kuhn, 1962/1970, 1977).

Now, it is reasonable to hold that the most influential and powerful currents of Anglo-American philosophy and psychology, particularly in the late nineteenth and twentieth centuries, have been strongly attracted to something very much like the unity of science program. In the context of the philosophy of psychology, theories tended to be assessed in terms of avoiding any and all forms of Cartesian dualism and of deviating from the explanatory canons of physics. At the present time, serious doubts have been expressed about the adequacy of the unity of science program for the physical sciences themselves. Furthermore, it has become clear that what we are to understand by a psychological property cannot be satisfactorily decided merely by reference to the methods of the physical sciences or to whatever physical properties may rightly be taken to be; and that resisting the theory that the mental and the physical signify utterly different kinds of substances or materials or compositional "stuffs" (*Cartesianism,* or *Cartesian dualism*) does not entail treating mental properties as merely physical or refusing to distinguish between the two. Perhaps, for instance, *having a thought* or *feeling a pain* is not just the same phenomenon as *being in a certain brain state,* even if the mental does depend on or involve (in some sense) being in a certain brain state.

In any case, it is not now normally maintained that the mere admission of real properties not reducible to physical properties—for instance, informational properties, functional properties, linguistic properties, cultural properties, as well as narrowly mental properties—entails a commitment to Cartesian dualism. Hence, it is not now usually maintained that a *nonreductive materialism* (a materialism that makes such concessions) is a contradiction in terms. For this reason and for convenience of reference, we may distinguish between *ontic dualism* and *attribute dualism* (Margolis, 1978a), that is, between a dualism of substances (most prominently, Cartesian dualism, a dualism of mind and body as the separate "materials" or "stuffs" that particular things are composed of) and a dualism (or pluralism) of properties or attributes (signifying only that entities of some internal complexity, though perhaps *composed* entirely of matter, are capable of exhibiting qualities, properties, and relations that cannot, in principle, be characterized in purely physical, or material, terms).

With this distinction in mind, we may characterize as a form of *materialism* any doctrine that: (1) opposes ontic dualism and (2) treats all particular things either as entirely composed of matter or as "linked" in some special way to whatever is entirely composed of matter. The vagueness of the term *linked* is deliberate; there may be a variety of relations involving objects, other than identity, so that to admit that there are things that are themselves not entirely composed of matter (but not composed of any "stuff" other than matter) need not threaten the materialist thesis. For example, words and sentences are not, in any familiar sense, composed of matter, although when used or uttered they are obviously (ontologically) "linked" in some complex way to sounds or physical marks that can be analyzed entirely in terms of material composition. The distinction is a strategic and subtle one, because materialism (as characterized) may take a reductive form (for example, *physicalism,* in accord with Feigl's extension of the concepts and laws of a "physical$_2$" science to the phenomena of biology and psychology) or a nonreductive form (still to be specified).

The principal question that concerns us here, of course, is whether persons, sentient animals, intelligent machines, art and artifacts, language, institutions, and actions can be (ontologically) analyzed consistently with materialism; and whether, in being thus analyzed, they may or must be construed reductively or nonreductively. Generically, materialism concerns only the issue of ontic composition (and of relations that do not adversely affect the resolution of that issue); whereas the qualifications "reductive" and "nonreductive" concern only the issue of whether the properties or attributes of things can or cannot be analyzed entirely in physical$_2$ terms—terms favored by the unity of science program or the like. "Materialism," therefore, opposes ontic dualism; and "reductive" and "nonreductive materialism" constitute, respectively, doctrines unfavorable and favorable to attribute dualism. *Functionalism,* for example, which attributes abstract, nonphysical properties to intelligent humans and computing machines—or else attributes certain complex properties "topic-neutrally," that is, without commitment to materialism, Cartesian dualism, or the like—need not thereby deny the tenability or adequacy of materialism, although how the two may be reconciled will require close study.

The idea, therefore, that materialism can admit ontological relations other than identity and composition, and the ascription of attributes other than physical or material, entails that materialism and physicalism are not equivalent doctrines and that functionalism (which we shall examine in Chapter 4) and physicalism are opposed concerning the possibility of attribute dualism. Peter Strawson's theory of persons (1959), for example, is probably the most famous version of a nonreductive materialism (committed to attribute dualism) that recent Anglo-American philosophy has devised. But Hilary Putnam's well-known early version of functionalism (1960) is another clear candidate. Strawson's theory introduces a relation other than composition and identity in order to account for the nature of persons. And Putnam's theory introduces attributes that cannot be defined physically but are generically compatible with materialism.

The adequacy of materialism can hardly be more than a provisional concession. Whatever eventually will prove to be the best account of the microtheoretical "materials" out of which the things of our world are composed may require an adjustment in what is currently termed materialism;

we need not presume to anticipate what basic science will eventually yield. On the other hand, the recent history of attempts to analyze psychological properties has tended to favor certain formal comparisons between humans and machines or else the purely formal features of human language. As we shall see in subsequent chapters, this tendency has not gone uncontested. But we may take notice here of a certain natural expectation regarding the adequacy of any theory of psychological properties, drawn for instance from the very caution Feigl expresses in urging a scientific account of the cognitive work of human scientists themselves.

Feigl is of two minds: He presses the need to accommodate conceptually the real psychological life of human investigators, but he also anticipates that physical_2 concepts will prove adequate to the task. The economy he favors is largely due to an influential proposal advanced by Wilfrid Sellars (1963), in which linguistic phenomena are not construed as *descriptive* of the actual psychological life of humans but treated rather as collecting social roles, conventions, intentions, and the like *that may be added externally to the scientific study of human beings in order to formulate our conception of what it is to be a human person.* In Sellars's sense, therefore, the linguistically significant, social behavior of human beings simply does not fall within the purview of science:

> To say that a certain person desired to do A, thought it his duty to do B but was forced to do C, is not to *describe* him as one might describe a scientific specimen. One does, indeed, describe him, but one does something more. And it is this something more which is the irreducible core of the framework of persons (p. 39).

In this view, such linguistic and psychological characterizations are entirely formal ("strictly logical," Sellars maintains), not descriptive of anything actual—that is, only *heuristic* as far as the scientific study of psychological reality is concerned. We treat the features in question as a mere *façon de parler* if we suppose we are inquiring into what bona fide science would countenance as real. Once we admit, however—ironically, with Feigl himself—that humans actually have a linguistic ability, have the power of actual speech and of other psychologically and culturally rich talents, we may fairly insist that the full experience and behavior of humans must be acknowledged as at least initially eligible for explanation *within* the competence of an adequate science. Language may perhaps be construed as an abstract system of some sort, but *linguistic ability* itself can hardly be denied as much psychological reality as pain or sensory perception.

It may be that some form of materialism (what, as we shall shortly see, is termed *eliminative materialism*) may justifiably reject mental phenomena as utterly illusory or the misleading posit of some distorting trick of language; but there can be no plausible presumption against the bare admissibility of the mental as requiring explanation. Sellars nowhere shows that psychological phenomena are not actual phenomena—within the range of things that science must account for. He secures the "closure" of the physical sciences simply by excluding the psychological and cultural as initial data. To refer to human persons, then, is, for Sellars, to refer to social roles or functions that we merely *assign* to what is real; but recalling Feigl's own caution, concern about $physical_1$ phenomena, Sellars fails to consider what may be entailed in *our* actually assigning such functions.

EXTENSIONALITY

We see, therefore, the strong conceptual linkage between ontological and methodological forms of reductionism—as well as the strategic importance of the usual range of psychological phenomena. *If* the psychological or mental cannot be ontologically reduced or eliminated in accord with a $physical_2$ vocabulary, then some form of attribute dualism must be conceded; and if that concession affects the analysis of such concepts as causality, causal laws, causal explanation, and the like, then substantive adjustments in the methodology of science may well be required. This caution explains the enormous appeal of the unity of science program and of similar programs that favor some form of so-called *extensionalism* or the extensionality thesis. However difficult it may be, the extensionality thesis is one of the most characteristic and one of the most globally favored in the philosophy of science. The advocacy of physicalism, it must be said, does not as such entail the extensionality thesis (see Carnap, 1937). In fact, it may even be incompatible with it, if for instance, as in Feigl's (early) formulation, physicalism is thought to depend on some ineliminable use of $physical_1$ phenomena (the experience of inquiring scientists).

Nevertheless, however much of a will-o'-the-wisp it may be, there can be little doubt that, as in the work of Rudolf Carnap (1937), W. V. Quine (1960), Wilfrid Sellars (1963), Donald Davidson (1967a), and Nelson Goodman (1951/1966), the extensionality thesis is very much favored in (it may even be the single most distinctive theme of) twentieth-century Anglo-American philosophy. In Carnap's terms (1937), the thesis argues that "*a universal language of science may be extensional;* or more exactly: For every given [nonextensional] language S_1, an extensional language S_2 may be constructed such that S_1 may be translated into S_2" (p. 245); or, in Quine's and Sellars's terms, "may be justifiably replaced by S_2."

We cannot at this point in our discussion hope to clarify satisfactorily the use of the terms *extensional, intentional,* and *intensional.* But very roughly speaking, a language is said to be *extensional* if:

1. in its sentences, the substitution of codesignative expressions does not alter the truth-value of the resultant sentences when compared with that of the original;

2. for its compound and complex sentences, truth-values are a function only of the truth-values of its constitutive clauses;
3. for those clauses, the substitution criterion is satisfied.

For example, the sentence *Tom believes that Cicero denounced Catiline* fails to satisfy the first two conditions although it satisfies the third: First, conceding that Cicero is identical with Tully (which Tom may not know or believe), the substitution of "Tully" for "Cicero" cannot insure the preservation of truth (*Tom believes that Tully denounced Catiline* may not be true); second, the entire (complex) sentence is not truth-functionally dependent on its constitutive values (*Tom believes that Cicero denounced Catiline* may be true whether *Cicero denounced Catiline* is true or false); nevertheless, third, the substitution of "Tully" for "Cicero" in the embedded clause preserves the truth-value of that clause (if *Cicero denounced Catiline* is true, then so also is *Tully denounced Catiline*). Sentences are said to behave *intensionally* if any of these conditions fails to obtain, the worry being that sentences about so-called *intentional* phenomena—that is, sentences about beliefs, fears, desires, conjectures, memories, dreams, and the like—behave intensionally, contrary to the presumption of extensionalism. *If*, then, sentences about inten*t*ional phenomena may be shown to behave extensionally, the admission of the intentional need not disturb the extensionality thesis. It is, however, widely supposed that sentences about intentional phenomena (prominently, if not exclusively, the mental) behave inten*s*ionally, that is, nonextensionally.

Here, we begin to see the point of Feigl's and Sellars's worries. The admission of psychological phenomena within the scope of science threatens to admit phenomena (so-called intentional phenomena) systematically recalcitrant to the extensionalist methodology of the physical sciences. Put most simply and in terms already introduced, *if* physical_1 phenomena cannot be reduced in physical_2 terms, extensionalism is bound to fail—with important consequences for the theory of what a science is, whether psychology is a science, and what kinds of properties actually characterize real things. Carnap himself (1932–1933/1959) had, very early in the career of the famous Vienna Circle, made the following bold pronouncement:

> Every sentence of psychology may be formulated in physical language . . . all sentences of psychology describe physical occurrences, namely, the physical behavior of humans and other animals. This is a sub-thesis of the general thesis of physicalism to the effect that physical language is a universal language, that is, a language into which every sentence may be translated.

Clearly, Carnap's physicalism does not correspond entirely with Feigl's. This may well be the most explicit manifesto of all the extensionalist programs of science from the beginning of the 1930s down to our own day. But it must be said that although Carnap never abandoned the thesis, neither he nor anyone else has ever shown how it could be successfully applied in a detailed way.

Quine has maintained that in the context of psychology, intensional sentences can be eliminated. He means that there are formal strategies for reinterpreting the structure of sentences involving verbs of "propositional attitude," like "believe that" (sentences about so-called intentional states), so that (though they remain inten*t*ional) they cease to behave *intensionally* (Quine, 1960). Nevertheless, Quine fails to show how, for instance, the extensional reading of *Tom believes that Cicero denounced Catiline can* be provided independently of our first knowing what is referred to in the clause following "believes" (see Margolis, 1977b). To know that *Of Cicero and Catiline, Tom believes that the first denounced the second* (the so-called extensionalist reading, in which mention of Cicero and Catiline does not first fall within the scope of what Tom believes), one must surely *first* know that Tom has a certain belief *about* Cicero and Catiline (the so-called intensionalist reading). Thus, either the extensional replacement fails because it depends inextricably on the intensional reading, or else the intensional reading is entirely compatible with the scientific prospects of psychology. Sellars is not sanguine, as Quine is, about the extensional treatment of sentences regarding psychological phenomena. For that reason, as we have seen, he tries to eliminate the psychological ("intentional discourse") from the legitimate range of the empirical sciences.

We shall turn very shortly to the concept of intentional phenomena. For the moment, we may construe, roughly, the mental as the intentional. The various strategies for "eliminating" the mental, then, may be said to depend on the analysis of the intentional. This is why the admission of the mental is such a fundamental challenge to the ambitions of science and the philosophy of science. The *only* alternative conceptual strategies available, *once the mental is admitted to be real and irreducible* in the respect considered, are: (1) that there can be no science of psychology or of social or cultural phenomena and (2) that if psychology and the cultural disciplines are bona fide sciences, such sciences cannot conform with any version of the unity of science program. The first alternative would generate a conceptual scandal; the second may entail a number of heterodox notions.

THE PRINCIPAL REDUCTIVE STRATEGIES

The principal strategies for reducing the mental, intentional, or psychological to the physical include the following:

1. equivalence or synonymy;
2. strict identity;
3. theoretical identity;

4. conceptual replacement;
5. elimination.

We shall begin our examination with the last method.

It should be said at once that these strategies need not be entirely independent of one another. Certainly, the baldest version of elimination in the psychological literature appears in J. B. Watson's somewhat startling early essay, "Psychology as the Behaviorist Views It" (1913/1963). There, Watson claims, "One can assume either the presence or the absence of consciousness anywhere in the phylogenetic scale without affecting the problems of behavior one jot or one tittle." What Watson meant, as he argues elsewhere (1925), was that psychology (the science of behavior) could achieve a satisfactory explanation of all the phenomena with which it was rightly concerned without introducing any mental concepts—relying solely on the concepts of physiology. Watson simply dismissed consciousness. In doing so, however, he never actually explained why he thought psychology could ("successfully") do without consciousness or what that really meant. Hence, he was roundly criticized both by that vigorous contemporary opponent of behaviorism, William McDougall (1913), who took introspection to be an ineliminable psychological method of limited use (that yielded information about sentient experience and conscious purposes), and by the so-called "neorealist," E. B. Holt (1931), who actually identified consciousness with neural phenomena (cf. Boden, 1972). Watson himself oscillated between simply dismissing consciousness as falling outside the strict constraints of the science of psychology and treating it *epiphenomenally* (that is, as caused, but not playing a causal role itself).

The crudity of Watson's program aside, the dismissal of mental concepts by elimination has, in our own time, been attempted in a variety of ways, particularly by Anglo-American philosophers. Sometimes, it is maintained (see Brodbeck, 1966; Körner, 1966) that mental concepts simply have no place in *causal* explanations—and hence, no place in science. In effect, this was also Gilbert Ryle's view. Ryle (1949) nowhere denies that mental states are real; he "merely" affirms that the mental *idiom* (properly) addresses itself to issues utterly unlike those of causal explanation. More extreme versions of elimination, however, are also in evidence. For example, in the postscript to his well-known *Essay,* Herbert Feigl (1958/1967) turns against his earlier view—that "there is an indispensable place for 'acquaintance' and 'knowledge by acquaintance' [this is, at least, sensory experience, the phenomena described in a physical_1 vocabulary] in a complete and adequate epistemology," hence in empirical psychology; he now supports elimination by way of conceptual replacement. Feigl holds a relatively "soft" view of elimination (replacement), for he insists that "nothing important is omitted in [the requisite] description." In fact, "the ascription of raw feels [phenomenal or sensory experience] to other persons is achieved in the scientific language by the ascription in terms of successor concepts of a specific 'structure' in the conceptual network of $physical_2$ science to a certain region (of $physical_2$) space-time"; "within the conceptual frame of theoretical natural science [he claims] genuinely phenomenal (raw feels) terms have no place" (pp. 141–142).

Feigl and J. B. Watson both believe (though for different reasons) that mental concepts must be eliminated from science. Feigl offers the more interesting objections. Although he is tempted by epiphenomenalism, he is utterly opposed to so-called interactionism; for in his view *interactionism* would be tantamount to admitting causal connections between a material and an immaterial order of things (Cartesianism or ontic dualism). On the other hand, though it need not entail the inadequacy of "$physical_2$ determinism," epiphenomenalism still leaves us (Feigl holds) with "nomological danglers" (in effect, explanatory lacunae: concepts of phenomena requiring scientific explanation that fail to identify such phenomena in ways that permit them to be subsumed under covering laws, for example, phenomenal descriptions of colors—*qualia*—thought to be neither translatable by, nor extensionally equivalent to, $physical_2$ descriptions of the phenomena in question).

The reason is simply that epiphenomenalism requires "a one-one correlation of Ψ's [mental phenomena] to (some, not all) Φ's [physical phenomena] with determinism (or as much of it as allowed for by modern physics) holding for the Φ-series"; the Ψ series is "far too spotty" to be deterministic in itself and not clearly enough linked with physical states and processes to permit its full incorporation within a larger physical theory (hence, the danglers). In his latest version, therefore, Feigl objects to mental states for two reasons: (1) because of the problem of nomological danglers and (2) because he now feels that suitable "successor concepts" (replacement concepts) can be introduced to link psychology to the needs of the unity of science. The appeal to "successor concepts" is openly intended to obviate the need for insuring either the translatability of mental terms by physical terms or the extensional equivalence of mental and physical ascriptions. The usual justification offered argues that the diachronic development of the sciences requires discontinuous changes in descriptive and explanatory concepts and characteristically exposes the relatively distorting or rough and approximate nature of earlier conceptual schemes that influence the formulation of present scientific claims (see Feigl, 1958/1967; Feyerabend, 1975; Kuhn, 1962/1970; Sellars, 1963). Hence, the appeal to "successor concepts" is available both to those who advocate elimination of the mental and to those who advocate a version of the identity theory.

CONCEPTUAL REPLACEMENT AND ELIMINATION

Here, precisely, we confront the vulnerability of conceptual replacement and elimination. For if there is reason to think that mental phenomena are actual—therefore, ineliminable—and also, not reducible to the physical, we should have to acknowledge both that sentient creatures are not physicalistically reducible and that psychology may not fall within the methodological canon prescribed for the physical sciences. But that is just the force of combining Sellars's admission of the irreducibility of the intentional and Feigl's (early) admission that at least the experience, the psychological experience, of working scientists ($physical_1$ phenomena) is quite real and subject to scientific explanation.

Still more extreme versions of elimination are possible. Some hold that only the physical is real, that what we purport to describe in mental terms is not real at all (so-called *eliminative materialism*). In Paul Feyerabend's view (1963a, 1963b), for instance, talk about the reality of mental experiences involves deep ideological bias (or mistaken theories) embedded in ordinary usage; in Richard Rorty's (early) view (1965, 1970a, 1970b), talk of the mental is simply a misguided way of talking of the physical, where one genuinely (but wrongly) supposes the mental to exist.

The accurate characterization of these views is difficult. Rorty now (1979) rejects "eliminative materialism"—by which he understands Feyerabend's view (and Quine's) but not his own. He takes the thesis to entail at least the denial of the following claim: "Some statements of the form 'I just had a sensation of pain' are true." This entails (for the eliminative materialist) that *it is false that we ever have mental states* (and that there are mental entities). Rorty opposes treating the mental in terms of mental *entities;* but he does not—as he once did (1970b)—support the eliminative materialist position. He now construes the problem of the mental or of consciousness as exclusively an epistemological one, disengages it from all would-be ontological questions, and insists that it can be decided by settling the question of the possibility of indubitable knowledge or "privileged access." The "elimination" of the mental, therefore, follows the rejection of the indubitable. No other issue remains. Nevertheless, like Sellars before him, he views personhood in terms of how the members of a society *treat* one another—that is, as a matter of decision among them, not of recognizing some common nature. Hence, he fails to see that *that* they really do decide entails an ontological question—however shorn it may be of its original Cartesian form or of the errant habit of treating the mental as the activity of *the* mind. As we shall see, in Chapter 4, the issue profoundly affects the fortunes of functionalism.

The admission of the mental, then, is the admission of a real, relatively unanalyzed range of salient phenomena, which traditionally have been thought to exhibit certain uniform properties or "marks"—for instance, *immateriality, abstractness, indubitability, privileged access, intentionality, phenomenal properties, introspectability, privacy*. But, contrary to Rorty's view, even if the mental fails to exhibit any such "marks" uniformly, it would not follow that the concept of the mental had no logical import or that the mental could be accounted for solely in epistemological terms. For instance, to deny, say, that pains are real *entities* is simply not to deny that some creatures really *feel* pain: The ontological status of mental properties remains a genuine issue. Similar considerations point to the arbitrariness of Ryle's precluding the causal interaction of the mental and the physical: The issue of interaction need not depend on the anomalies of the Cartesian ontology; it remains a perfectly straightforward empirical question. Does pain cause wincing? Can a physical blow cause pain? Even the self-styled dualist (see Eccles, 1970; Penfield, 1965; Sperry, 1969) may not actually subscribe to a full-blooded Cartesian theory and may merely intend to affirm that: (1) on the available evidence, or in principle, reductive materialism (all five strategies) is implausible or indefensible; and/or (2) independently considered, there is, *contra* elimination at least, good evidence of mind/body interaction.

A more telling objection against elimination is also a more humble one. It is simply a fact—a stunning, ubiquitous fact—*that we use* our idiom of mental terms *in order to report our sentient experiences* (see Cornman, 1968a, 1968b). It may well be that pains and sensations are not entities, particulars of any sort (Rorty's charge); but the fact is that we take ourselves to be able to report—and do report—our experience of pain, our sensations, our images, our thoughts and beliefs and intentions. To explain *these* can hardly be to suppose that they are not real or genuine, and to "replace" them in the sense said to favor the progress of science is simply to provide a substitute idiom *that must (and will inevitably) acquire the original reporting role of the first idiom,* unless, on independent grounds, it can be shown that eliminative materialism is genuinely effective.

But there seems to be no way to *show* that. As long as there is any sense in admitting introspective reports (without regard to indubitability), there is no conceivable way of sustaining the radical eliminative position; and there is no way of conceiving creatures that acquire a *natural* language—that acquire a language naturally, by growing up among the linguistically apt members of their own species—without assigning them an introspective capacity. On any plausible view, the acquisition of language in infancy entails *some* capacity for thought, belief, intention, desire, affect, perception, and the like. J. B. Watson's original proposal, therefore, merely to ignore mental concepts in fashioning psychological explanations is quite preposterous; and the direct, radical elimination of such concepts, quite impossible.

Hence, conceptual replacement cannot rightly be subordinated to the purposes of elimination and, given the recalcitrance of mental phenomena, must be linked rather to the fortunes of some version of equivalence, strict identity, or theoretical identity. Sellars's theory is perhaps the most sustained effort to oppose this conclusion. In the argument advanced, however, the advocacy of (physical) "successor" concepts for the mental (Sellars's term) must (plausibly) represent a somewhat more relaxed program for achieving a reductive materialism than the strict requirements of either identity or extensional equivalence would permit. In short, conceptual replacement could conceivably be justified *if* there were evidence strongly favoring some version of equivalence or strict or theoretical identity, in spite of the fact that the independent confirmation of elimination proved impossible or unworkable. The most reasonable basis for supporting conceptual replacement lies with the alleged imprecision, distortion, partial irrelevance, and even superstition of our historically contingent ordinary language (what Sellars, 1963, terms "the manifest image"). There is some justice in the charge. But the "replacement" of introspective reporting itself hardly follows. Sellars's theory threatens the existence of the very scientist or philosopher who advances his theory—in threatening his real capacity to report his views. We cannot, therefore, as yet ignore or deny the ordinary and obvious features of the psychological:

1. that the behavior of the inquiring scientist itself constitutes data for the science of psychology;
2. that the scientist's behavior and that of "specimen" humans are essentially similar;
3. that the explanation of observed human behavior presupposes that the observing scientist and the scientist's subject share in a consensual way culturally shaped practices and aptitudes (see Apel, 1972/1980).

We shall return to these issues at the very end of our account.

IDENTITY AND EQUIVALENCE

Strategies of equivalence and strict or theoretical identity are peculiarly defective. First, there are almost no important theorists who hold that the sentences of the mental idiom are either synonymous with or translatable into those of a canonical physical idiom (equivalence). Among philosophers, Thomas Hobbes perhaps comes as close as any to believing that, for example, sensation (correspondingly, imagination, thought, and other mental distinctions) can be rendered as "some internal [mechanical] motion in the sentient [body]" (*De Corpore*); but Hobbes offers no details and is noticeably silent about the analysis of the intentional and epistemological aspects of mental phenomena. As remarked earlier, Carnap affirms the translation thesis but never pursues it. Among modern psychologists, C. L. Hull's (1943) theoretical intentions are perhaps most vigorously in sympathy with the effort. Hull maintains that although the mental phenomena involved in the intelligent molar behavior of humans are real enough, the concepts of such phenomena have a *deductive* relation to the terms of a strictly mechanistic language (cf. Spence, 1956)—hence, are completely expressible in those terms. It may come as a surprise to some that Freud, particularly in the *Scientific Project* (1895/1966), provides one of the most valiant and sustained efforts to formulate the translational connections between a mental and a neuronal language, though the development of his clinical work appeared (to Freud himself) to thwart that objective (see Margolis, 1978b).

The leading materialists attracted to the identity of the mental and the physical hold, as does J. J. C. Smart, in his justly famous article (1959/1962), that synonymy fails, that translation is impossible, and that, nevertheless, selected sentences from the mental and physical idioms may be shown, on empirical grounds, to be equivalent in truth-value. That this is not sufficient for the identity thesis, Smart himself freely concedes. Through a number of discussions of the issue, however, Smart (1963) betrays a certain telltale oscillation regarding whether the identity theory is actually an empirically confirmable claim or only an intelligible "metaphysical" claim—and not, therefore, actually empirically confirmable. Spinoza's system may be taken as ample confirmation that identity is not deductively entailed by Smart's conditions; and Smart himself has been explicitly challenged along just these lines (see Brandt & Kim, 1967).

The problem is compounded, since if equivalence is rejected or weakened to mere extensional equivalence, then what is usually called "strict identity" is impossible to demonstrate. Strict identity requires conformity with what is loosely characterized as Leibniz's law—a strong extentionalist constraint to the effect that codesignative terms may be substituted in all linguistic contexts, *salve veritate* (preserving truth). The difficulty posed by Leibniz's law is simply that no one denies that some linguistic contexts are unalterably intensional, so that the substitutivity of codesignative terms often fails to preserve given truth-values; moreover, these intensional contexts are characteristically just the ones in which the identity theory is supposed to be tested. For example, given the actual pattern of ordinary discourse, if a pain is described as "searing" or "throbbing," or if "having a throbbing pain" is predicated of a particular person, one would have difficulty specifying what (kind of) physical state (a state of neural discharge?)—hence, which particular physical state—could be described as "searing" or "throbbing," or what (a physical body?) would be said to "have a throbbing pain," before actually confirming the identity theory itself. Again, we have no established way of deciding whether, say, *Tom believes that Jack and Jill went up the hill* conveys the same belief as, or a different belief from, *Tom believes that Jill and Jack went up the hill,* or which of these (or other logically equivalent or entailed propositions) could be said to be identical with which neural states or the like (see Armstrong, 1973). We cannot be certain of the numerical identity of given beliefs specified in alternative intensional ways, though we can imagine circumstances in which we could plausibly hold that they were the same or that they were different (for example, as in the difference between adults and children who have not yet mastered the commutative convention regarding "and" in "Jack and Jill"). But we have no way at all of specifying such beliefs by independent, extensional criteria—in particular, by purely physical criteria—or of ascribing such beliefs in an extensionally routinized way to systems identified in purely physical terms. Leibniz's law, therefore, must have an extremely limited bearing on establishing or disconfirming the identity theory.

Formally, *strict identity* is often rendered thus:

$$(x)\ (y)\ [(x = y) \supset (F)\ (Fx = Fy)].$$

(That is, for every particular thing x and every y, if x is identical with y, then for every property F, F may be truly predicated of x if and only if F may be truly predicated of y.) But this can never be demonstrated if synonymy or translation fails to obtain; for then, mental and physical properties cannot always be even meaningfully *ascribed* to the same things (that is, to *whatever* is identified as x and as y). The regularities of ordinary linguistic usage produce an interference phenomenon. There arises, therefore, an antecedent difficulty regarding what Jerry Fodor (1968) has called the Law of Transferable Epithets: If "Fy" does not even make sense, where "Fx" does, then identity cannot be demonstrated in accord with Leibniz's law; although that failure does not entail a failure of identity as well, unless, on independent grounds, it can be shown that every true identity must be able to be shown to satisfy Leibniz's law. If, say, pains cannot be assigned physical location in the same sense in which neural discharges can (even though a locational idiom is used in connection with how pains feel—"I feel a pain in my left upper molar"), then it would be impossible to identify pains with neural discharges *by* invoking Leibniz's law.

The fact is that Leibniz's law captures the familiar (and very strong) intuition regarding identity: that what is true of a thing is true of it, no matter how it may be designated. We seem to lack a better formal representation of identity; and there are no known constraints that we could impose on linguistic contexts that in a reasonable and non-question-begging way, would permit Leibniz's law to hold well enough where pertinent claims of strict identity were thought most clearly valid. For example, suppose we precluded (for purposes of testing strict identity) all sentential contexts in which (1) sentences embedded in other sentences were (2) prefixed by so-called "verbs of propositional attitude" (*believe, know, fear, hope, wish,* and the like). As we have seen, such contexts do not conform to Leibniz's law: If the sentence *Tom believes [knows, fears] that Cicero denounced Catiline* is true, then, in spite of the fact that Cicero is identical with Tully (one and the same man is rightly designated by either name), it *may* be false (it certainly does not follow *deductively*) that *Tom believes that Tully denounced Catiline* is true. After all, Tom may not know or believe that Cicero = Tully. The fact that it may be so (and need not be self-contradictory) is decisive. The sense in which the substitution of the codesignative name *Tully* for *Cicero* does not preserve truth is just the sense in which: (1) the first sentence may be taken to report the propositional content of what is "in Tom's mind"; (2) the *embedded* sentences may be taken to be equivalent in truth-value; and (3) the second sentence, judged solely *on the basis of the first,* cannot also be taken to report what is in Tom's mind. Here, then, we have a clear example of the inten*s*ional complexity of inten*t*ional contexts. Furthermore, in this example, we have clear evidence that we cannot impose any useful constraints on the application of Leibniz's law for the purpose of testing the identity theory; the cases we should want to test by appeal to Leibniz's law are the very ones we should have to preclude in order to insure extensionality.

There *is* a sense, of course, in which, if Tom believes that Cicero denounced Catiline, he believes that Tully denounced Catiline; that is, he believes *of a certain man* (alternatively identified by *us* as Cicero or Tully) that that man denounced Catiline. But that is a sense in which, precisely, we ignore the crucial part of what, on the first reading, we take to be the content of what is in Tom's mind. In particular, we cannot then admit that the sentence *Tom does not believe that Cicero = Tully* is or could be true, self-consistent, and consistent also with the truth of the sentence *Tom believes that Cicero denounced Catiline.* But that seems to preclude a genuinely empirical possibility. Also, the formula offered impoverishes what, *ex hypothesi,* is Tom's belief, that is, that *Cicero* denounced Catiline, not that *a certain man* did.

The extensionalist strategy for analyzing such belief-sentences has been most forcefully pursued by Quine (1960) and is closely related to his particular version of the strategy of elimination. What Quine shows, correctly, is that reference (in our example) to Cicero and Catiline must be construed "transparently," that is, in a way *not* governed (prefixed) by the verb (or "operator") of propositional attitude ("believes that")—in effect, not governed intensionally—*if* an extensionalist canon for the whole of science is to be vindicated. The trouble (as we have seen) is that Quine examines the question exclusively in a formal way; but the concern of science cannot be separated from the methodological and epistemological issue of *how,* precisely, to replace the intensional ("opaque") idiom, *Tom believes that Cicero denounced Catiline,* by the required extensional one—for instance, as by offering *Of Cicero and Catiline, it is true that Tom believes that the first denounced the second.* As we have seen, Quine's maneuver is to fix the reference to Cicero and Catiline *outside* the scope of the verb *believes that;* he thereby replaces an "opaque" (intensional) context with a "transparent" (extensional) one.

In fact, the very prospect of replacing the intensional idiom by the extensional one, in the context of a working science, encourages us to believe that science *can* actually function in an acceptable way by using the original intensional idiom; otherwise, there would be no basis for confirming its canonical replacement. But *if* that is so, then it must be true that sciences may be rightly characterized as such *even if a comprehensive extensionalist replacement for all intensional idioms proves impossible* (see Margolis, 1977b). This is why the canon of the unity of science program cannot, once and for all, be taken to be definitive of all bona fide sciences. It remains an empirical issue (in effect, it is so regarded by Quine himself) whether the extensionalist program can actually be carried out.

The difficulty of the undertaking shows as well the reasonableness of invoking a replacement strategy where a strict synonymy cannot be shown to obtain. Quine has always (1953) opposed even the coherence of claims of that sort. Hence, we see the relevant sense in which Sellars's and Quine's strategies tend to converge and are jointly blocked by the same recalcitrance of the mental. Ironically, the upshot is that just in the sense in which we seriously entertain the extensionalist program, we must provide for the conceptual possibility that heterodox theories of the nature of science may actually be vindicated—that is, by demonstrating (with greater force than the advocacy of the unity of science and of related programs can expect to muster) the failure, or the likelihood of failure, of sustained and systematic efforts to replace (or eliminate) those intentional phenomena central to the psychological and cultural disciplines themselves. If they resist extensionalist replacements, we should have to reconsider the methodological properties of such sciences as psychology, quite apart from any idealized account of science we may happen to favor.

INTENTIONALITY

Mental states corresponding to the verbs of propositional attitude are normally said to be *intentional*—similarly, the verbs and even the sentences are said to be intentional—because the states in question are said to be "about" or "directed upon" the thoughts (or "propositional objects") that the embedded sentences represent, or because they are simply said to be "about" objects in some sense that does not require the existence of "those objects" (see Brentano, 1874/1973; Chisholm, 1957). (In the original medieval idiom, such "objects" were said to be "intentionally inexistent.") Since Leibniz's law characteristically does not hold in intentional contexts, such sentences are said to behave *intensionally* as well. As we have seen, Quine construes such sentences *extensionally* (although they remain intentional). But this shows, very clearly, that we must provide a sense (which extensionalism itself requires) in which the inten*t*ional need not behave intensionally; for otherwise, the strategies of replacement and elimination could only be pursued in the most radical way, which is empirically premature and conceptually dubious. This may suggest why Quine is attracted to *both* an extensionalist reading of belief-sentences and an extreme form of eliminative materialism. But they are not the same or equivalent undertakings.

In effect, we must take note of the difference between the *intentional* and the *intensional.* The intensional is a purely linguistic distinction or a linguistically grounded distinction, whereas the intentional is not, a matter of considerable importance; for if the intensional is an attribute of language or of linguistically informed systems—cultures, for example, artifacts and cultural phenomena that depend on the work of linguistically apt agents—then intensional puzzles *cannot* arise with respect to the psychological states of languageless animals or cannot arise in the same way in which they do for linguistically apt humans.

It is relatively easy to demonstrate that not all sentences involving intentional (mental-state) verbs (or verbs of propositional attitude) behave intensionally; some—notably, Quine (1960)—have argued that there are, also, sentences that behave intensionally that do not involve intentional verbs at all. For example, regarding the former case, if *John is thinking of [about] Alaska* is true, then, by substitution, so also is *John is thinking of [about] the largest state of the United States* (see Cornman, 1962b; Margolis, 1977a). Notice that the sentence is neither compound nor complex. It cannot, therefore, be shown to be intentional in accord with that criterion (illustrated by the Cicero/Catiline example and favored by Brentano) with which the truth or falsity of the embedded sentence is indifferent to the truth or falsity of the embedding sentence. And it is not intentional according to another well-known criterion (also advanced by Brentano), namely, that its truth is indifferent to the existence or nonexistence of the object "intended." The substitution of *the largest state of the United States* for *Alaska* does seem to depend on the existence of Alaska, whereas *Tom is dreaming about unicorns* and *Ponce de Leon searched for the Fountain of Youth* appear to behave intensionally, precisely because the "intended" objects are imaginary. It appears, then, that the Alaska case is intentional based on the criterion (not supplied by Brentano, more in accord with the views of Edmund Husserl) that to be conscious or aware of something real (as in perception) is still to be "directed" (to "intend" that object) (see Brentano, 1874/1973; Husserl, 1931; also, Føllesdal, 1969).

On the other hand, rightly or wrongly, Quine holds that sentences like *Necessarily, 9 is greater than 4* behave intensionally, although they are not in any obvious sense intentional. His reasoning is that since 9 = the number of the major planets, then, by substitution, it should be the case that *Necessarily, the number of the major planets is greater than 4* is true; but it is false. (Their number might have been smaller.) It would take us too far afield to explore his claim, though Quine sees affinities between such sentences and the structure of indirect discourse, which is itself closely related to the analysis of Tom's holding a belief about Cicero and Catiline (see Geach, 1957; Kenny, 1963). The important thing, here, is that the intensional and the inten*t*ional are quite distinct notions, that the second is primarily a psychological category (and only secondarily a linguistic one), and that the first is primarily a linguistic category (and serves as a psychological or cultural category only on the assumption that linguistic abilities are psychological as well).

Brentano had confused issues a great deal by his account of intentionality, particularly because he intruded inten*s*ionality as a third criterion of inten*t*ionality. Furthermore, his first two criteria (as we have just seen) do not yield isomorphic results and cannot always be jointly invoked. Sometimes, what is intentional on one criterion (indifference regarding existence and nonexistence) actually behaves extensionally, not intensionally at all. Also, if Quine is right, intensional contexts need not involve the mental at all (though Quine's argument may well depend on a critical equivocation). Again, *contra* Brentano, the intentional (as in thinking about Alaska, seeing a dog, flogging a horse—but not as in searching for the Fountain of Youth, fearing goblins, hunting for lions) may be directed to what is actual only.

The inten*t*ional, then, appears among languageless animals as well as humans—or, by extension, among machines; but the inten*s*ional applies only to language, linguistically generated phenomena, or cultural artifacts produced by linguistically apt agents, or the behavior and psychological powers of human beings. We may, therefore, usefully introduce an additional term of art, the *Intentional,* by which we shall mean phenomena regarding the mental states and behavior of linguistically (*a fortiori,* culturally) apt agents *and* regarding what, thus qualified, such agents produce, generate, or make (see Margolis, 1980). Here, the Intentional may be roughly rendered as the "rule-governed" ("rule-following" or "rulelike"). Their salient features, however, must include: (1) the inten*s*ional ("description-relative") characterization of what falls under a given rule (institution, practice, tradition, or the like) and (2) the possibility of altering operative rules and their purpose—hence, also, the intensional characterization of what falls under the altered regularities. Consequently, *I*ntentional phenomena need not be psychological in nature, although their existence depends on the activity of *i*ntentionally (psychologically) qualified agents. The principal conceptual advantage afforded by *I*ntentionality is simply that it permits the attribution of linguistically and culturally significant properties to the activities and production of social groups, without supposing that such properties are always psychologically applicable (or psychologically "internalized") with respect to particular human agents. For example, it is conceivable that a musician composes a piece of music that on a fair interpretation is construed as baroque; but it does not follow that the musician must have generated his music in a psychologically pertinent way in accord with the (Intentional) uniformities of the baroque. It may well be the case that such uniformities *cannot* have been completely internalized psychologically. We shall return to this theme in the final chapter, in examining the prospects of what has been called cognitivism.

FORMS OF THE IDENTITY THEORY

We need to say more about the forms of the identity theory. Here, discussion follows at least two distinct lines of thought: first, what may be said about identity if Leibniz's law is viewed either as false (because of important counterinstances) or as too weak to decide the matter (because, properly restricted in the way in which it is taken to be true, it precludes application to the troublesome cases of mental phenomena that we wish to decide); second, what may be said about identity distinguished in what has come to be called its "type" and "token" versions.

The strategy of *theoretical identity* simply maintains that mental phenomena are (identical with) physical phenomena, for theoretical reasons that do not depend on applications of Leibniz's law. Often, its advocates (see Cornman, 1968a, 1968b) hold that efforts to demonstrate identity via Leibniz's law are doomed to commit a category mistake: that the actual use of terms or predicates may be restricted on linguistic grounds, without touching on the issue of identity; and that such constraints preclude (as in Ryle's bifurcation of the idioms of the mental and physical) the mixing of mental (or physical) predicates and descriptive and referential expressions identifying things in physical (or mental) terms. Nevertheless, according to the argument, *what* is specified and *what* is attributed to it, cast in alternative mental and physical idioms, are one and the same. Such identities are said to be *cross-category identities*. Logically, of course, they are strict identities. There are no identities but strict identities: What is identical with itself is necessarily identical with itself (although the existence of no natural thing is thereby insured). The notion of a "theoretical identity," then, is simply the notion of a strict identity, regarding the confirmation of which Leibniz's law is denied application.

There are difficulties with this theory. For one thing, "theoretical identity" is often made to follow as a matter of ontological economy from the alleged extensional equivalance of paired mental and physical attributions. That is, if the correlations obtain, then, as a matter of parsimony (Smart, 1963), what is thus related must (it is said) be identical. The *non sequitur* is clear. This suggests (see Brandt & Kim, 1967) that there are conceptual alternatives to identity consistent with such equivalence, and hence, that the relative force of reductive and nonreductive possibilities must be explicitly compared.

Second, the paradigms of cross-category identity offered in the empirical sciences (lightning bolts and aggregates of ionized particles, gases and aggregates of molecules) are invariably drawn from purely physical phenomena (see Cornman, 1962a; Feigl, 1958/1967; Smart 1959/1962). One simply cannot find an acknowledged canonical instance of a cross-category identity involving the mental and the physical that plays an explanatory, law-governed role in any science comparable to that played by the physical paradigms mentioned. The upshot is that it is simply unclear *what* criteria or conditions should be taken to establish a psychophysical identity.

Third, although it is often taken for granted that we may at least establish the requisite empirical correlations between the mental and the physical, the fact is that under the usual conditions adduced, it is demonstrably impossible for just those phenomena that do not lend themselves to vindicating Leibniz's law. For consider that where "propositional attitudes" obtain (*believing that, fearing that, wishing that*), intensional puzzles regarding identity, individuation, and reidentification also obtain. If, then, physical phenomena may be specified in extensionally effective ways and if the relevant mental phenomena *cannot,* then it is impossible to establish the requisite sorts of empirical correlations or equivalences *in virtue of which* contingent claims of theoretical identity may be said to afford an ontological economy. All the advocates of theoretical identity (for instance, Cornman, 1962a; Feigl, 1958/1967) fail to see that there is no effective way in which to establish such correlations.

To speak of psychophysical *correlations* is, effectively, to speak of "type" identity theories, of theories that maintain that the occurrence of mental phenomena of certain types can be correlated as such (causally or noncausally) with the occurrence of physical phenomena of certain types. But if mental and physical phenomena cannot be isomorphically specified because of intensional problems (see Davidson, 1970; Fodor, 1975), then either (1) empirical correlations can at best be approximated by indefinitely extended or infinite disjunctions (both methodologically unmanageable), or else (2) the effort at type identity is conceptually impossible. The first possibility is the result of Feigl's and Cornman's concessions; and the second (as we shall see) leads promisingly in the direction of functionalism. In short, there is every reason to believe that *the individuation of mental and physical states is based on quite different principles.*

Here, we may anticipate an important development. For if, (1) mental phenomena are real, (2) causally efficacious, and (3) *not* identical with physical phenomena, then either we cannot avoid ontic dualism or we must provide an alternative way of construing the mental. Now, *all* versions of the identity theory—type and token versions—concede both the first and second statements; and these are precisely what are resisted (in various ways) by *all* forms of eliminative materialism. One sees why, therefore, if type identity theories are unconfirmable, token identity will appear as a last defense for certain theorists committed both to the adequacy of an extensionalist program *and* to the truth, on commonsense grounds, of both statements. This is just the motivation for Donald Davidson's well-known theory of *anomalous monism* (1970), in effect, the principal formulation of the *token* version of mind/body identity. If, however, token identity fails—that is, the third statement is upheld, *and* if the first two statements remain true, then the defeat of the identity theory must threaten the gravest consequences for the methodology of the psychological and cultural sciences. In particular, for instance, it may become necessary to concede that at least sometimes, causal contexts may (*contra* Davidson, 1971) behave intensionally rather than extensionally (beliefs, for example, may be causally efficacious, but on the grounds adduced, identifiable only in intensional terms); and that at least sometimes, causality need not (again, *contra* Davidson, 1970) entail nomologicality (that is, causal connections, if specifiable only intensionally, *could* not be shown to fall under covering laws). This explains a good part of the appeal of eliminative and reductive programs. Here, we are simply taking notice of what is at stake.

Type identity differs markedly from token identity in that it is: (1) committed to the discovery of causal laws covering types of mental events and (2) committed (at least in the most developed versions) to the feasibility of identifying mental events extensionally *prior* to testing identity claims themselves. The best known specimen of such a view is the one advanced by J. J. C. Smart (1959/1962). Its novelty lies with Smart's having introduced the strategy of a "topic-neutral" identification of mental phenomena (cf. Levin, 1979). In effect, Smart is a "cross-category" identity theorist persuaded that the mental can be extensionally specified without characterizing it in *either* mentalistic *or* physicalistic terms (that is, he holds that it may be characterized *topic-neutrally*). Without the success of such a maneuver, the empirical prospect of the first commitment is essentially zero. In various ways, well-known causal theories of the mental (see Armstrong, 1968; Lewis, 1966; Pitcher, 1971) are keyed to something like Smart's strategy, particularly in that they seek to eliminate reference to the phenomenal distinction of the mental (to sensations, images, feelings, and the like). Such reductions must fail, however, if the topic-neutral maneuver itself cannot succeed. And it cannot—for demonstrable reasons.

Smart's proposal addresses itself essentially to the topic-neutral treatment of phenomenal qualities of the mental rather than to what is explicitly intentional. Replace all reference to the phenomenal, it recommends, in accordance with the following formula: "When a person says, 'I see a yellowish-orange afterimage,' he is saying something like this: '*there is something going on which is like what is going on* when I have my eyes open, am awake, and there is an orange illuminated in good light in front of me; that is when I really see an orange.'" But the formula is not satisfactorily explained. For one thing, Smart elucidates the sensory qualities of sensory perception "as powers, in Locke's sense, to evoke certain sorts of discriminatory responses in human beings"—that is, in topic-neutral terms as well. But it is not clear how, in empirical terms, suitable type regularities of this behavioral sort can be reliably ascribed in a non-question-begging way to, say, all discriminable colors. Second, Smart elucidates the putative qualities of sensations, afterimages, and the like solely by matching their powers to evoke certain sorts of discriminatory responses with counterpart discriminatory responses already (dubiously) assigned to veridical perception. Hence, he holds that the behavioral dispositions in the two cases are *like* one another. But he nowhere explains the *respect* in which "what is going on" in the one case is *like* what is going on in the other, *in virtue of which the alleged similarity in behavioral responsiveness can itself justifiably be thought to fix the mental event involved, without any attention to phenomenal qualities at all.*

It seems, therefore, either impossible to perform the feat without invoking distinctions that are not topic-neutral or hopelessly question-begging to claim to be able to. In fact, Smart actually states that "the strength of [his thesis] depends on the possibility of our being able to report that one thing is like another without being able to state the respect in which it is like." The trouble is that *in reporting* that having an afterimage is like seeing an orange, and so on, one *is* referring to the *phenomenal respect* in which (however, vaguely or imperfectly) the first is *like* the second. (Otherwise, we should be driven to define the phenomenal in behavioral terms.) If the objection is a fair one, we cannot allow Smart's claim to have supplied an extensional (topic-neutral) identification of types of mental phenomena in virtue of which strict type-identity claims may be confirmed. Both on empirical and conceptual grounds, it seems extremely farfetched to suppose that there is some set of discriminatory dispositions that could be empirically relied on to pick out, extensionally (in a topic-neutral way), what we should otherwise have to specify in phenomenal (intensional) terms. For one thing, there are no known regularities that link *qualia* and behavioral dispositions; and for a second, the behavioral dispositions in question are bound to be individuated *by* reference to intentional considerations that bear once again on phenomenal discriminations. How, otherwise, should we ever discount mistakes and discrepancies of all sorts regarding seemingly promising correlations?

Regarding token identity, we should notice straight off that the difficulties in applying Leibniz's law, the topic-neutral identification of the mental, and the provision of reasoned criteria for affirming cross-category identities apply with equal force to both type and token theories. In fact, one of the most telling constraints affecting token identity is that to affirm the thesis entails affirming the empirical possibility of type identity as well. (The entailment is often resisted.) It is just the distinction of Davidson's version of token identity (certainly the best known and best developed) that it precludes that possibility. Based on the argument, therefore, token identity must fail as well. Of course, token-identity theorists need not subscribe to Davidson's argument. For example, they may hold that although psychophysical laws are entirely possible (see Stevens, 1957), supporting evidence is too weak to be relied on, or there may be no known such laws on which to rely; hence, causal explanations involving the mental may not involve more than token identities (see Fodor, 1975).

Davidson's theory (1970) is committed to the consistency of the following triad and to the truth of its constituent propositions:

> (i) at least some mental events interact causally with physical events (the Principle of Causal Interaction); (ii) where there is causality, there must be a law: events related as cause and effect fall under strict deterministic laws (the Principle of the Nomological Character of Causality); (iii) there are no strict deterministic laws on the basis of which mental events can be predicted and explained (the Anomalism of the Mental).

It is clear that in being committed to the "anomalism of the mental," Davidson opposes the supporters of type identity in denying—consistently with their joint acceptance of the reality and causal efficacy of mental events—"the existence of psychophysical laws." *Anomalous monism,* then, signifies the conjunction of this denial and the affirmative claim that "all events are physical." Hence, the defeat of token identity—conceding the reality and causal efficacy of the mental—cannot fail to affect the methodology of the sciences concerned with mental phenomena.

Now, Davidson explicitly insists that "the mental is nomologically irreducible: there may be *true* general statements relating the mental and the physical, statements that have the logical form of a law; but they are not lawlike. . . ." Unfortunately, he nowhere explains precisely how to decide whether true general statements about the mental are or are not lawlike; and so he cannot, at least as far as the formal properties of laws are concerned, claim that general statements linking the mental and the physical cannot be lawlike.

Also, Davidson holds that "lawlike statements are general statements that support counterfactual and subjunctive claims, and are supported by their instances"; but it is not clear that all general statements supporting counterfactual and subjunctive claims are lawlike. Regularities said to be "cosmic accidents" or accidental regularities with a long run of luck that are not (or would not happen to be) disconfirmed by particular finite sets of test cases appear to support counterfactual and subjunctive claims as well as normal, lawlike claims (for example, such claims as *If that [or that] radiator had frozen, it would have broken;* or *If that [or that] piece of butter had been heated to 150°F., it would have melted*). The relationship between the antecedent and consequent of all such conditionals may not be one that marks a lawlike propensity or trait, even though the occurrence of the event specified by the *consequent* will normally be open to causal explanation (for example, *If that [or that] chicken gizzard has an odd number of stones in it, war will break out*). Only if one refused to concede such a possibility—for instance, by holding that only the assumption or denial of lawlike propensities underlying such regularities affects the admissibility of supporting such claims—could one hold that only lawlike generalizations actually support counterfactual and subjunctive claims (see Goodman, 1955/1965; Stegmüller, 1977). But that would beg the question at stake; and it is a maneuver that Davidson in effect denies himself.

In fact, Davidson admits that "there is (in my view) no non-question-begging criterion of the lawlike," that "lawlikeness is a matter of degree. . . ." Also, he admits that (ii) is "stronger than required"; in fact, it is clearly contrary to familiar views about probabilistic laws (cf. Salmon, 1970). With these distinctions in place, it is relatively easy to see that just as with Smart, Davidson's token-identity thesis requires some topic-neutral way of treating the mental extensionally. But if that *is* possible, then the type-identity thesis is also eligible. Hence, the triad is inconsistent, since (iii) is incompatible with type identity. That is, if (i) is true, then, in principle (in Davidson's view), mental events must fall under covering laws (ii). But if they do, then it is impossible to preclude psychophysical laws for conceptual reasons alone (iii).

Hence, the triad is inconsistent. It is impossible, in short, that if individual mental events can be suitably identified as such—so that they can be known to enter into causal relations—they cannot (in principle) enter as such into nomological relations. If mental phenomena can be assigned a causal role, they can be identified in a suitably extensional way; and if, as such, they can be identified extensionally, they can enter into lawlike relations. Thus, either the mental cannot as such be assigned a causal role (which Davidson denies), or psychophysical laws are conceptually and empirically possible (which Davidson also denies). But these alternatives are exhaustive as well as exclusive, *and they do not depend on either token or type identity.* In fact, Davidson emphatically says that "causality and identity are relations between individual events no matter how described" (that is, they hold extensionally).

Davidson offers a further, entirely plausible basis for construing discourse about the mental intensionally: The "attribution of mental phenomena," he says, "must be responsible to the background of reasons, beliefs, and intentions of the individual"; our particular ascriptions are progressively adjusted to accumulating evidence controlled and interpreted by reference to "the constitutive ideal of rationality." This means that generalizations about reasons *cannot* be lawlike because (1) they are "indefinitely refinable" relative to description-relative considerations, and (2) they are thus refinable in terms of a "holistic" grasp of the interrelationship among all relevantly specified elements. In effect, this means that the mental is incorrigibly inten*s*ional. If so, then either the mental cannot be assigned a causal role (because of the extensionality of causal contexts), or if it is assigned a causal role, the psychological and cultural sciences cannot be treated methodologically in the same way as the physical sciences (because intensionally specified causes cannot, as such, be said to fall under covering laws). Furthermore, if the mental is incorrigibly intensional, then all forms of the identity theory must fail (because no isomorphism and no manageable correlations could obtain between the mental and the physical).

There appear to be no further alternatives within the framework of reductive materialism. We are obliged, then, to move on.

CHAPTER THREE

Behaviorism

THE CHALLENGE OF BEHAVIORISM

We have rejected various forms of reductive materialism for both ontological and methodological reasons. But it is quite impossible to regard the argument as settled without a close examination of the varieties of behaviorism. In fact, from the behaviorist outlook, to have conceded the primacy of cognitive psychology within the entire range of the social and behavioral disciplines may already be questionable. Certainly, for extreme behaviorists—notably, B. F. Skinner—the concession is thought to encourage, if not to entail, the false doctrine that psychological explanations require an ineliminable reference to internal mental states.

Skinner, of course, has been the most energetic and influential behaviorist in the Anglo-American tradition. He is critical (1938, 1974) of both J. B. Watson and I. P. Pavlov, for instance, and, somewhat more implicitly, of Clark Hull's motivational and drive theories (influenced by Pavlov) involving ineliminable central "need states" (Hull, 1943); and he is particularly attentive to the philosophical and conceptual problems that the science of psychology poses. He objects to Watson's blithe neglect of psychological states and stresses his failure to distinguish, both conceptually and methodologically, between behavioral and physiological accounts. He objects to Pavlov's and Hull's reliance on central states, and to E. C. Tolman's characterization of central states in mental and intentional terms. Norman Malcolm (1964) applauds Skinner's exposure of the "error of introspectionism," that is, that "psychological reports and utterances . . . are based on observations of inner mental events"; but he also objects to Skinner's "error of behaviorism," that is, that psychological ascriptions are based entirely "on observations of outward events or of physical events inside the speaker's skin." Nevertheless, the putative "error" is indeed the methodological clue to Skinner's entire program as well as to the central philosophical challenge that behaviorism poses. It turns out, therefore, that the principal conceptual issues to be raised regarding behaviorism may all be conveniently reviewed in the process of reviewing Skinner's own work.

Within the range of modern learning theory (see Hilgard & Bower, 1975), the principal American views have tended to center on two themes:

1. whether relevant explanations of behavior can be adequately provided in terms restricted to such factors as stimuli, responses, and reinforcement schedules, or whether they require reference to central states (cortical and subcortical states, as in physiological psychology);
2. whether intentional or mentalistic characterizations of either or both behavioral and central-state elements may be defensibly eliminated in the interest of bringing psychology into closer accord with the physical sciences.

The Skinnerian orientation takes a strong position both against the explanatory importance of central states and in favor of reducing or eliminating the intentional. By contrast, the Pavlovian view requires central states and though favoring the adequacy of a physiologically grounded vocabulary, does not actually address the issue of systematically replacing reference to "subjective states"—particularly at the human level—by the use of an essentially physiological vocabulary (see Pavlov, 1927, 1928). The polar alternatives of the first theme serve, also, to fix the essential difference between Pavlov's so-called "classical conditioning" (the "conditioned response") and Skinner's so-called "operant conditioning" (in which "emitted" behavior does not depend on some *immediately* provided stimulus).

The fundamental difference between Pavlov and Skinner remains, of course, the difference between a physiologist and a psychologist. Pavlov holds reductive views about the mind/body problem, but these have rather little place in his detailed study of the conditioned reflex and appear, primarily, in his polemical remarks. Skinner also has reductive convictions, but these, precisely, are directly addressed to the analysis of mental phenomena. Hence, Skinner's view of the first theme is only partly directed against Pavlov: Physiologically characterized central states do not (Skinner claims) bear on the explanation of behavior, although they have a genuinely explanatory function; but central states characterized in mental terms have no explanatory function at all. The difference between the two is often obscured by construing the entire range of behavioristically oriented theories as *stimulus-response* (S-R) theories. But the important difference, in the context of psychology, has more to do with the greater theoretical importance assigned to the second theme than to the first. In any case, the resolution of the first theme—as, for instance, favoring Pavlov—need not entail the resolution of the second. Nevertheless, the first raises conceptual issues of importance (see Estes, 1958; Spence, 1956).

We may say that the essential conceptual issue that behaviorism poses for the philosophy of psychology concerns the eliminability of mental terms (and their referents, of course) from causal accounts. In that sense, the challenge of behaviorism is at least methodological; although, in a realist interpretation of explanation, such elimination can hardly fail to have ontological import as well. It is not important, therefore, in the present context, to attempt to appraise or formulate alternative versions of behaviorism, once behaviorists concede—if they do, say, in the manner of E. C. Tolman (1958)—that mental states may be ineliminably required in psychological explanation. On the other hand, to admit mental states at the explanatory level must have consequences for the characterization of psychology as an empirical science.

ALTERNATIVE FORMS OF BEHAVIORISM

Behaviorism is not one doctrine. Skinner himself has changed his view from time to time, has commented on the versions he rejects and favors, and has even classified certain alternative forms of behaviorism. In the most convenient classification, there are said to be at least three significantly different fundamental versions: (1) *logical* (or philosophical) *behaviorism,* (2) *methodological behaviorism,* and (3) *radical behaviorism* (see Lacey, 1978; also, Kaufman, 1967; Mischel, 1975). Skinner is often described as a logical behaviorist; but it may be more accurate to identify him as a radical behaviorist. He does say (1974) that "mental life and the world in which it is lived are . . . invented on the analogy of external behavior occurring under external contingencies" (p. 115), which suggests one version of logical behaviorism; but notably in his disapproval of J. B. Watson's psychological program, he makes it quite clear that merely to ignore mental and psychological phenomena is neither to reject the introspectionist's appeal to inner states *nor* to preserve the behavior to be explained. He also says, "I consider scores, if not hundreds, of examples of mentalistic usage. . . . Many of these expressions I 'translate into behavior'" (1974), which suggests another version of logical behaviorism. More characteristically, Skinner (1974) regards the effort at translation as peripheral to the explanatory efforts of psychology, in accord with which "states of mind . . . may be interpreted as collateral products of the contingencies which generate behavior" (p. 75)—a version of radical behaviorism.

Logical behaviorism maintains that all mental predicates (or descriptive and explanatory terms) may be translated, paraphrased, defined, analyzed, reduced, eliminated, or replaced by behavioral and environmental terms, without any loss in the power to designate whatever is psychologically real. Logical behaviorism is simply the counterpart of various forms of reductive materialism. It may be fairly said that Skinner nowhere completes a specimen account of such a reduction. But Skinner himself explicitly affirms that he is "a radical behaviorist simply in the sense that I find no place in the formulation [of psychological explanations] for anything which is mental" (Wann, 1964).*

Methodological behaviorism is equivocally characterized by Skinner, depending on whether he intends his own or J. B. Watson's practice to illustrate the notion. It is, in any case, a theory about the methodological constraints properly imposed on, and the explanatory powers of, empirical psychology. If we take Watson as the paradigm, then methodological behaviorism is simply the behaviorist counterpart of those materialist views that preclude the mental from even falling within the explanatory competence of empirical science (mentioned in the preceding chapter). If we take Skinner as the paradigm, then methodological behaviorism is the methodological face of radical behaviorism—which we have yet to characterize. In this second sense, "while there may be regularities involving cognitive variables [in effect, mental states], any data which supported hypotheses concerning them also would support hypotheses about [nonmentalistic] environmental regularities (which are deducible from the cognitive hypotheses)" (Lacey, 1978). At any rate, we can accommodate the intended distinction, while emphasizing (what Skinner insists on) that behaviorism need not, and does not, ignore the mental.

Radical behaviorism maintains (Skinner, 1953) that "from (1) that behavior occurs as a function of cognitive variables, and (2) that the cognitive variables are functions of environmental variables, it can be deduced that the behavior occurs as a function of environmental variables" (Lacey, 1978); *and* that, because of this, explanations in terms of cognitive variables are entirely vacuous and mental phenomena are fictions. The argument is a *non sequitur,* in the sense that if there are independent functional laws covering the first proposition and independent functional laws covering the second, there may not be any such laws covering the conclusion. The variables identified in both propositions need not be logically related in such a way as to permit any lawlike conclusion. This need not, in fact, represent the radical behaviorist's best view. For if the replacement of mental terms need not involve "exact behavioral equivalents," the radical behaviorist need only maintain that "the objection to inner states is not that they do not exist, but that they are not relevant in a functional analysis" (Skinner, 1953); that states of mind are only "collateral products of the contingencies which generate behavior" (1974, p. 75): that "mentalistic

*A quoted comment of Skinner in the exchange following the discussion of his paper (1964), at a symposium in the Rice University Semicentennial series.

explanations explain nothing" (1974). Part of Skinner's intent is to claim the adequacy of explanations of behavior in environmental (and genetic) terms; and part, to insist on the vacuity of explanations restricted to inner mental states.

Skinner's reasons may strike us now as rather naive. For one thing, he sees (1974) the admission of the mental, the purposive, the volitional, the intentional as entailing some form of ontic dualism; though distinguishing (as we already have) between ontic and attribute dualism, it obviously need not. For a second, Skinner (1964) appears to rule out the full relevance of introspection on grounds weakly linked to his views of the "empirical." For a third, he (1974) seems to believe that mental processes "are real enough at the level of behavior, but merely questionable metaphors when moved inside [to facilitate explanation]." But the behavioral analysis of the mental is not explicitly supplied; the claim that the mental occurs only in manifest behavior appears (on introspective grounds) to be flatly false; and the imputed vacuity of explaining behavior in terms of central psychological states is, thus far, merely a question-begging charge. Finally, Skinner opposes the explanatory use of inner mental phenomena because they are "unobservable" and "inferred," hence incapable of explaining behavior (1953). Nevertheless, they are introspectively accessible and publicly intelligible, and observational data about behavior itself may support in an empirical way reference to inner mental states (fear, say, on the basis of apparently fearful behavior) that need not be completely accessible, even introspectively.

OBJECTIONS TO BEHAVIORISM

The most serious questions confronting behaviorism include at least the following:

1. whether the mental can be described in terms not logically dependent on the behavioral;
2. whether the entire range of behavior can be described in nonintentional or nonmentalistic terms;
3. whether the explanation of behavior, or at least of a significant range of behavior, can be satisfactorily provided without reference to inner or central mental states;
4. whether it is an open question, given behavioristic criteria of intelligence or the like, that a system, satisfying such criteria, may still be said to lack a mind.

All four lines of inquiry have been amply explored in the literature.

The most inclusive negative response on the first question—in effect, mounting an attack on logical behaviorism—is probably furnished by Fodor (1968). In Fodor's view, the behaviorist accepts the following as a necessary truth: (*P*) "For each mental predicate that can be employed in a psychological explanation, there must be at least one description of behavior to which it bears a logical connection" (p. 51). Fodor intends the expression "logical connection" to be not restricted to purely deductive connections; if, for instance, one admits a "criterial" or "grammatical" connection between the mental and the behavioral—as in Wittgenstein's (1953/1963) famous remark "An 'inner process' stands in need of outward criteria"—one maintains a behaviorist position. Fodor dubs those who deny "necessarily *P*" *mentalists;* hence, mentalism is not equivalent to dualism, and with behaviorism, exhaustively and exclusively classifies all psychologists. Also, mentalism is compatible with (but does not entail) monism, and in particular is compatible with (but does not entail) materialism. In effect, mentalists (Fodor, 1968) hold that "statements about minds and statements about behavior are logically independent" (p. 56). The strongest sense in which mentalists may support their claim is simply in affirming that *mental events may be the causes of behavioral events;* for in any standard view, events that are causally connected (say, a feeling of panic and running) are contingent and independent of one another. Behaviorists can defend their position only by establishing the affirmative view regarding the third question (whether the explanation of behavior can be satisfactorily provided without reference to inner or central mental states) *and* by showing that inner mental phenomena are themselves behavioristically construed—in effect, by demonstrating the validity of logical behaviorism.

Provisionally, then, unless causal interaction is untenable, behaviorism risks an easy defeat—as in the commonsense admission that pain may cause one to wince. Notice that Skinner does appear to acknowledge mental causes of behavior. He cannot simply hold that, *in their turn,* such causes are functions of environmental variables; that is, he cannot simply hold that the (mental) causes of behavior are themselves caused. That, effectively, would be to concede his opponent's position with respect to the first question (whether the mental can be described in terms not logically dependent on the behavioral), since it would entail the independence of mental events and behavior. Independent central mental states would then be impossible to deny. Skinner must hold, as he apparently intends, that reference to the mental is no more than a convenient idiom for approximating, by stages, genuinely operative causes—the lawlike connections (holding solely) between behavior and environment. That thesis, however, is precisely the one in dispute.

Again, it is no weakness that mentalism entails (as Fodor remarks) a commitment to "minimal skepticism," that is, to the view that we cannot, on the basis of observable behavior, determine with logical certainty which mental state one is in; the fact is that a behaviorism in which only criterial or grammatical connections between the mental and the behavioral hold is already committed to minimal skepticism—the result, simply, of admitting that criteria are sufficient only in some idealized context that never actually obtains (see Albritton, 1959; Malcolm, 1954). In order, therefore, for Skinner to conform to his own restricted view of what is observable (in which physical objects and physical movements are the paradigms), he must opt for some form of logical behaviorism. Connections as loose as the criterial would entail a fundamental revision in Skinner's notion of what, within the context of empirical science, is actually capable of being observed. On the strength of our earlier counterarguments against reductive materialism, logical behaviorism would seem impossible to establish.

Regarding the second question (whether the entire range of behavior can be described in nonintentional or nonmentalistic terms)—and, somewhat less directly, the third—the principal objection has been posed by Roderick Chisholm (1957), namely, that every effort to secure a behavioral analysis of mental states (in particular, believing and intending) either fails or smuggles in an ulterior intentional distinction that is overlooked. In effect, in Chisholm's view, intentionally qualified phenomena cannot be adequately characterized in terms of physical movements alone. Charles Taylor (1964) adds the following important claim: that "the distinction between action [that is, cognitively directed behavior] and movement [involves] the notion of a center of responsibility which is inseparable from the notion of action" (pp. 56–57); "what is essential to this notion of an 'inside,'" he adds, "is the notion of consciousness in the sense of intentionality," that is, that one's action "has an intentional description for him, is an 'intentional object'" (pp. 58–59). This holds, not unreasonably, for human beings, who, after all, are linguistically apt.

Taylor provides more routine evidence of the difficulty in holding the affirmative with regard to describing behavior in nonintentional terms. He observes that "it is a peculiarity of an action that its having a given direction or being an action of a certain kind is a fact which holds of it independently of the antecedent conditions which give rise to it. We first identify the action and then search for the conditions which brought it about" (p. 45). *If* an action cannot be identified as an action in virtue merely of any set of finitely many physical movements, then we cannot hope to vindicate the behaviorist view of describing behavior in nonintentional terms. One way or another, we should be obliged to introduce controlling central states. For example, there seems to be no reasonable way in which to identify an act of insulting another—first or in general—by identifying a physical movement or set of alternative movements that have that intentional import; and to acknowledge its intentionality as psychologically real seems to require reference to the agent's central states.

Here, a complication arises, because there are alternative ways of describing central states that need not entail mentalism. N. Tinbergen (1951/1969), for instance, manages in his pioneer study of animal instinct to combine innatism and behaviorism—methodological behaviorism, perhaps—in a way that is strikingly in accord with Skinner's strictures on objective science (although critical of his avoidance of innately controlled behavior). Several issues need to be stressed regarding Tinbergen's work. In a spirit not unlike Taylor's, with regard to the higher mammals and man at least, Tinbergen does not oppose intentional ascriptions. But among his favored phenomena—within the range (say) of insects and birds—he says quite flatly that "although . . . the ethologist does not want to deny the possible existence of subjective [mental] phenomena in animals, he claims that it is futile to present them as causes, since they cannot be observed by scientific methods" (p. 5). Accordingly, they supply ("hunger" and "anger," for instance) "a *convenient description* of the state of the animal, based on subjective as well as objective criteria"; "they are," however, he says, "known only by introspection" (p. 5).

But the avoidance of intentional or cognitive ascriptions is and must be compensated for by characterizing effective stimuli (now thought to be identified in behavioristic or "objective" terms) *functionally*, that is, in terms involving something like recognizing an abstract or universal similarity among a set of concrete stimuli. In his famous studies of the stickleback, for instance, Tinbergen noted that the fighting of males during spring mating was probably triggered in such a way that "the fish reacted essentially to the red and neglected the other characteristics [of an opponent fish]. Yet its eyes are perfectly able to 'see' these other details" (p. 28). All his studies of ingenious changes in the size and shape of the decoy stickleback, in the distinctive red coloring around the throat and belly, and in similar features confirm that stimuli must be construed abstractly or functionally—as involving, in some sense, the discrimination of a determinate color as falling (say) within a range "programmed" for response. Similarly, "the reactions of many birds to flying birds of prey are often released by quite harmless birds": Tinbergen and Konrad Lorenz (1970) have tested the power of various quite differently shaped bird models to "release" the same relevant response.

In short, there is no way in which such a (teleological) model of explaining cognitive or noncognitive but purposive behavior can be sustained without admitting abstract, functional properties *both* in the description of behavior—pertinent to describing behavior in nonintentional terms—*and* in the characterization of central causes—pertinent to explaining behavior without reference to inner or central mental states. This, then, affects both Tinbergen's and Skinner's position in a most decisive way; for Skinner (as well as E. L. Thorndike, 1949, and Pavlov) is committed to the lawlike reinforcement of certain behavioral regularities. It makes no difference (in this regard) whether we are dealing with *classical* or *operant conditioning* (that is, with the difference, respectively, between conditioning in which contingent sensory stimuli evoke or elicit species-specific reflexes or responses, usually keyed to standard sensory events, and conditioning in which spontaneously "emitted" behavioral acts "operate" on the environment to reinforce a generalized behavioral response). In Skinner's view, it is the *operant* (the generalized behavioral response) that is reinforced by the presentation of a reinforcing stimulus. But the operant is a functionally or *abstractly* described response. It cannot be a class of determinate responses (although Skinner, 1938, seems tempted at times by that characterization), since a physical movement must be determinate and particular; but it cannot be a particular response either, since physical responses must differ fairly widely from instance to instance, and since it is simply false that reinforcing patterns (of any sort) reinforce any particular physical response. It must, therefore, be the abstract functional response that is reinforced and is the same from particular response to particular response. But if so, then Skinner cannot meet his own constraints on observationality.

Alternatively, if functional attributes are thus introduced, then Skinner cannot satisfy the behaviorist version of describing behavior either in nonintentional terms or without referring to central mental states; for to support the theory of operants even minimally, one would have to construe organisms as automata programmed to respond to a range of determinate stimuli (a view close to Tinbergen's). That would require the admission of central states at the explanatory level, though not necessarily mental states, which Skinner is at pains to avoid. In short, there is every reason to believe that the very concept of an operant is the behaviorist's obscure alternative to the mentalist's appeal to central states. The discrimination of functional or abstract similarities across a range of particular stimuli requires the admission of suitable central states in the discriminating system; if that ability is treated as cognitively significant, then those central states must be mental.

These considerations signify that even at an animal level below cognition, properties, dispositions, and capacities must be ascribed that:

1. cannot be defined or analyzed solely in physical terms (attribute dualism);
2. cannot be said to be "observationally" accessible in the behaviorist's sense;
3. must be linked with internal, central states of organisms distinct from their determinate behavior;
4. are defensible in terms of the actual empirical practices of science;
5. must play a causal role in the empirical explanation of actual behavior.

It is difficult to see, therefore, why analogous powers of a fully mental or cognitive sort should not, among the higher animals and man at least, be defensible for even stronger reasons. The argument bears as much on excluding central states as on using nonintentional terms, and introduces us to the initial plausibility of preferring functionalism (the topic of the next chapter) to behaviorism.

We may add, here, that there can be no effective behaviorist analysis of such statements as E. C. Tolman's "the rat expects food at location *L*"

(Tolman, Ritchie, & Kalish, 1946)—if we mean to capture anything like its ordinary sense. Tolman's definition of the rat's expectancy holds that

> . . . if (1) he is deprived of food, (2) he has been trained on path *P*, (3) he is now put on path *P*, (4) path *P* is now blocked, and (5) there are other paths which lead away from path *P*, one of which points directly to location *L*, *then* [the rat] will run down the path which points directly to location *L*.

Correspondingly, the rat's not expecting food at location *L* entails that under those conditions, "he will not run down the path which points directly to location *L*." But, say, "if there were a cat astride the path leading to *L*, we would not take the immobility or even retreat of the rat as evidence that he did not expect food at *L*" (Taylor, 1964, p. 80). The problem is precisely that of the adequacy of nonintentional criteria in intentional contexts. There simply is no finite set of Tolmanian conditions for testing whether an expectancy obtains or not.

THE EXPLANATION OF BEHAVIOR VIA INTERNAL STATES

We must look at the exclusion of central states more closely. The most famous criticism of Skinner, with regard to this question, is, of course, that offered by Noam Chomsky (1959) in his review of Skinner's *Verbal Behavior* (1957). Chomsky stresses the general inescapability of admitting internally organized dispositions toward learning or cognitive growth. Skinner opposes all such views, because he takes them (unjustifiably) to entail Cartesian dualism: "the theory of an invisible, detachable self . . . a little man or homunculus" whose "wishes . . . become the acts of the man observed by his fellows" (Skinner, 1964, p. 79). He also objects to the inherently "incomplate" nature of explanations given in terms of (central) mental causes. For instance, he says, "A disturbance in behavior is not explained by relating it to felt anxiety until the anxiety has in turn been explained. An action is not explained by attributing it to expectations until the expectations have in turn been accounted for." (As we shall see, in a later chapter, this issue will distinguish the *cognitivist* from the behaviorist.) Here, Skinner simply collapses the need to explain molar behavior into the charge that to do so by reference to central mental states is necessarily incomplete.

Chomsky attempts to demonstrate that verbal behavior could not be satisfactorily explained (or even described) in terms of Skinner's "functional analysis." The acquisition of language, he claims, is simply incompatible with Skinner's theory, emphasizing particularly the peculiar rapidity with which children learn to perform in a linguistically skillful way, and also, the "creative" feature of language, the fact that competent speakers can produce and understand sentences instantly that they have never produced or heard before.

Elsewhere, Chomsky (1957) argues that certain grammatical complexities of language (in particular, the "embedding" of sentences) are in effect inexplicable on the basis of the learning processes admitted by Skinner. His claim is that the processes of sentence formation (in natural languages) "have no finite limit," but (in effect) the reinforcement of operants requires "finite state processes." "English is not a finite state language" (p. 21), Chomsky maintains, in the sense that it cannot be accounted for by a system or machine that moves in a finite number of steps from an "initial state" to a "final state," *producing in each intermediate state an additional word.* Such a finite state language may be said to exhibit a "finite state grammar." But the embedding of sentences—for instance, "if S_1, then S_2," "Either S_3, or S_4," "The man who said that S_5, is arriving today" (where S_1, S_2, S_3, . . . are declarative sentences in English)—cannot be generated by a finite state grammar (p. 22). All such sentences will exhibit word dependencies (across the comma, in our specimen cases) that permit the insertion of *S*s, to produce infinitely many sentences. A finite state grammar cannot account for the rules by which an infinitude of such sentences can be produced or for the *dependency* constraint. *If* the reinforcement of verbal operants conforms to the inadequate power of a finite state grammar (which may be challenged), then Chomsky has indeed shown that Skinner's behaviorist account of language must fail. It remains true, nevertheless, that Skinner has not shown *how* operant conditioning can escape Chomsky's attack; and the operant model itself seems, on the evidence, not sufficiently articulated (see Lacey, 1974).

Furthermore, regarding the exclusion of central states in descriptions of behavior, R. J. Nelson (1969) has demonstrated that "a behaviorist-limited description is too weak to describe automaton performance"; hence, that *if* animals are automata (which Nelson accepts but does not demonstrate), then behaviorism is too weak to describe animal behavior. However, by analogy at least, Nelson does show that the explanation of animal behavior—*a fortiori,* higher-order behavior—requires the admission not only of inputs and outputs but of internal states as well. His essential claim is that internal states are not logically dispensable, as Skinner supposes. What Nelson shows is that a system may exhibit multiple dispositions that are not extensionally equivalent; hence, that multiple dispositions fail to "characterize internal states uniquely"; hence, that internal states are not reducible in dispositional terms or eliminable. But behaviorist descriptions are intended to collect such dispositions and to eschew internal states. Accordingly, the program must fail. Nelson also shows that internal states "are not definable in any way in terms of the language of neurophysiology, etc., on grounds that they are not physically identifiable in all members of a species in the same way." That two sets of persons are playing a game of chess, for instance, entails nothing about the physical moves they make; and that a person is in a state of expectation entails nothing, in a sufficiently determinate sense, about his or her physical states and movements.

Finally, D. M. Armstrong (1968) offers a conceptual argument against the behaviorist account of dispositions. First of all, Armstrong maintains (against the behaviorist) that dispositions may be ascribed to things even when they are not actually manifested; second, he argues that the behaviorist *cannot* have any explanatory basis for ascribing dispositions (or for predicting behavior) *except* that of the mere record of what has already happened on previous occasions. Behaviorism, therefore, confuses dispositions and states and fails to grasp the conceptual connection between central states and the abstractly specified dispositional uniformity of its various physical manifestations. His opponent, then, *has a conceptual basis for speaking of dispositions as "causal factors,"* because "an object's having a dispositional property entails [its being] in some nondispositional state" responsible for its "manifesting certain behavior in certain circumstances" (p. 86). In effect, Skinner cannot provide for the causal explanation of behavior, and though he may successfully predict behavior, he cannot do so on causal grounds. Hence, we must adopt a negative stance regarding the exclusion of central states.

BEHAVIORISTIC CRITERIA OF INTELLIGENCE

The standard argument regarding the question of intelligence is provided by C. D. Broad (1925), although he could not have been familiar with the most recent work regarding the machine simulation of intelligence. "However completely the behavior of an external body answers to the behavioristic tests for intelligence," Broad affirms, "it always remains a perfectly sensible question to ask: 'Has it really got a mind, or is it merely an automaton?'" (p. 614). (We should, today, admit the logical possibility of intelligent, mentally apt automata—conceivably, human beings themselves.)

The most recent compelling revival of Broad's approach appears in a paper by Ned Block (1981). Block subscribes to what he terms *psychologism,* the thesis that what makes behavior intelligent "depends on the character of the internal information processing that produces it." Hence, according to psychologism:

> . . . two systems could be exactly alike in their actual and potential behavior, and in their behavioral dispositions and behavioral capacities and counterfactual properties . . . yet there could be a difference in the information processing that mediates their stimuli and responses that determines that one is not at all intelligent, while the other is fully intelligent.

In effect, Block's view is a fresh version of Broad's claim, and clearly requires a negative view of using only nonintentional terms and excluding central states.

A. M. Turing (1950) originally introduced the well-known notion of an "imitation game," in accordance with which human interrogators could judge whether machines think and whether interrogators could always reasonably decide whether they were dealing with machines or humans. Block (1981) converts this game into the Turing Test of intelligence, taking care to avoid a strictly operationalist interpretation ("if a system is given the Turing Test, then it is intelligent if and only if it passes") and a "behavioral disposition formulation" (since passing may be accidental, failing need not indicate a lack of disposition, and human judges are too easily fooled by "mindless machines"). Block shows that "no behavioral disposition is sufficient for intelligence," and that if "intelligence is identified with a *capacity* [rather than a disposition] to produce sensible responses," behaviorism still remains inadequate.

On the "neo-Turing Test conception of intelligence . . . intelligence (or more accurately, conversational intelligence) is the capacity to produce a sensible sequence of verbal responses to a sequence of verbal stimuli, whatever they may be." Thus armed, Block describes an "unintelligent machine" that although it satisfies the test, is, because of its internal information processing, "conclusively" shown to be "totally lacking in intelligence." Imagine a machine, then, provided with a large finite set of sentences, of which a subset may be construed as a "sensible string" if and only if it is a conversation "in which at least one party's contribution is sensible." In principle, the (finite) set of sensible strings (sentences) could be listed by intelligent humans. The machine is confronted by a sentence offered from its original list. It then searches the set of sensible strings beginning with that sentence, picks one at random, and (in the story) types it out. The interrogator produces another sentence. The machine makes a selection from the subset of its sensible strings that begins with the first sentence and includes, sequentially, its first response and the second sentence of its interrogator. The game continues in that way. Whatever apparent intelligence the machine exhibits is, then, solely that of its programmers. Hence, Block concludes, even "the capacity to emit sensible responses is *not* sufficient for intelligence." Intelligence depends, at least in part, on the causal conditions under which it is produced—in effect, confirming the negative claim regarding the exclusion of central states by way of an affirmative claim regarding the lack of a mind (see Boden, 1977; Dreyfus, 1972/1979). One extremely convenient way of summarizing the thrust of the argument is simply to acknowledge that psychological terms—*think, add, conjecture, perceive, feel, intend, want, decide, know,* and the like—can be usefully employed in speaking of systems known to *lack* mental or cognitive powers, machines that merely mimic intelligent behavior, for instance.

At the very least, then, returning to our narrower issue, the principal forms of behaviorism appear inadequate to the tasks of an empirical psychology. Behaviorism seems unable to eliminate mental terms at either the descriptive or explanatory level and, in particular, seems unable to eliminate central mental states.

CHAPTER FOUR

Functionalism

FUNCTIONALISM CHARACTERIZED

Our arguments against reductive materialism and behaviorism are essentially designed to separate the analysis of mental and physical properties from the issue of accepting or rejecting Cartesian or ontic dualism. Ontic dualism is generally admitted to be utterly opposed to any view of a unified and continuous world that the sciences could favor. If reductionism and behaviorism are untenable, and if ontic dualism is conceptually intolerable, both are equally to be avoided. On the other hand, we need not suppose that distinguishing between mental and physical properties entails the objectionable doctrine. Still, *if* mental phenomena are (1) real, (2) really distinct from (not reducible to) the purely physical, and (3) capable of exerting causal influence, then dualism *is* compatible with these three propositions—though *not* in a way that yields admissible explanations in science.

Functionalism is the name usually assigned to theories that subscribe to these three propositions at least—*without either favoring or precluding dualism.* Sometimes, the term is also intended in a weaker sense, in which the usefulness of descriptions and explanations cast in mental terms is conceded, without addressing the question of whether the mental can be reduced to the physical or whether systems so described actually have mental properties. For example, it is extremely convenient, in anticipating the behavior of a machine programmed to play chess, to characterize the machine's "moves" in terms of the usual strategies open to a human opponent, without being committed to ascribing a mental life to the machine. Functionalism, then, takes either an explicit *realist* or a derivative *heuristic* form. Either way, it is intended to provide, in scientific contexts, as much flexibility (perhaps only provisional) as is needed in distinguishing between the mental and the physical, without explicit commitment either to ontic dualism or monism.

More generally, in the context of psychology, functionalism provides a theory of the *differences between* mental and physical properties rather than a theory of the nature of psychological explanation (Block, 1978). In this sense, counterpart forms of functionalism appear in the context of biology, machine behavior, animal psychology, and the so-called "human studies." The DNA molecule, machines, animals, artworks, and language are often said to exhibit functional as well as physical properties, in a sense not obviously the same as that used in speaking of human minds. Provisionally, the following may serve as examples of *functional* properties:

(a player) mating an opponent's king;
(the DNA molecule) coding a certain genetic development;
(a sculpture) representing the passion of Christ;
(the word *casa*) meaning *house* or *home*;
(a computer) calculating one's income tax.

We shall ignore here altogether the various senses in which, in the behavioral and social sciences, one speaks of functional *explanations*. B. F. Skinner (1974), for example, views his explanations as functional, though as a radical behaviorist he explicitly opposes functional properties, that is, opposes construing mental attributes as functional.

The issues that concern us center primarily on the analysis of mental and functional properties, and subsequently, on the bearing of that analysis on the methodology of the psychological, social, and cultural disciplines. We may anticipate a variety of views about the distinctive nature of functional properties, and these will surely occupy us in an important way. Still, there are two fundamental questions to be asked that will simplify matters enormously:

1. Are functional properties heuristically or realistically ascribed?
2. Are functional properties abstract properties or only abstracted from more complex properties?

Notice that wherever functional properties are only heuristically invoked (as in speaking of a plant's *searching for* nutrients by *sending out* its roots), we are ultimately bound to consider whether we favor some form of eliminative theory. Notice also that wherever functional properties are treated realistically *and* as abstract properties, we are inevitably committed to some form of ontic or Cartesian dualism. If so, then, assuming the intolerability of dualism, functionalism is either untenable or no more than an incomplete formulation of some more adequate theory of mental and functional attributes.

We may gain a better impression of the force of these two questions by considering the difference between some very perceptive but undeveloped views of C. D. Broad and some very highly developed views of Hilary Putnam. In attempting to account nonreductively for the causal role of the "mind" (so-called Two-sided Interaction), Broad (1925) insists that "the Conservation of Energy [principle] is absolutely irrelevant to the question . . ." (p. 104). *If* it were relevant, Broad believes, then either physicalism or dualism or radical behaviorism would have to be favored, since the distinct *energy* expended by the mental would have to be accounted for. The conservation principle "says . . . that, *if* energy leaves A, it must appear in something else, say B; so that A and B together form a conservative system." But the principle does not require that "if a change in A has anything to do with causing a change in B, energy must leave A and flow into B" (p. 107).

Broad presses two points here: First, the principle does not actually explain causal change; it only imposes limits on "the changes that are possible"; second, even in a physical system—in a pendulum, for instance—the string on which a weight is placed affects "the direction and velocity of the weight's motion," in spite of the fact that "the string makes no difference to the total energy of the weight." The first point is quite correct; the second may be better stated. What Broad means to draw attention to is simply that in alternatively structured energy systems, causal changes take alternative forms; and the *structures* of such systems are attributes abstracted from them in such a way that *they* cannot *as such bear causally* on the flow of energy. The abstracted structures are not causes, though alternatively structured material forces *are* causes; if merely formal or abstract structures were causes (could function as independent causes), we should have to acknowledge a nonphysical source of energy; hence, we should have to subscribe to some form of ontic dualism. "Why should not the mind act on the body in this way?" Broad asks, "If you say that you can see how a string can affect the movement of a weight, but cannot see how a volition can affect the movement of a material particle, you have deserted the scientific argument . . ." (p. 108).

Consider, now, the functionalism of Putnam (1967/1975a):

> . . . to know for certain that a human being has a particular belief, or preference, or whatever, involves knowing something about the functional organization of the human being. As applied to Turing machines [abstract computers 'with a finite number of internal configurations each of which involves the machine's being in one of a finite number of states' determined by the machine's scanning the discrete symbols of its tape (1960)], the functional organization is given by the machine table [that is, the complete instructions for being in any of its states]. A description of the functional organization of a human being might well be something quite different

> and more complicated. But the important thing is the descriptions of the functional organization of a system are logically different in kind either from descriptions of its physical-chemical composition or from descriptions of its actual and potential behavior.

This explains both why Putnam rejects "traditional materialism" (physicalism) and behaviorism and why he construes the mind/body problem as a full analogue of the functional state/physical state problem regarding Turing machines (1960).

Putnam's essential emphasis (1960) is that just as "a given 'Turing machine' is an *abstract* machine which may be physically realized in an almost infinite number of different ways," and which is "completely described" in terms of a purely abstract machine table specifying its ("logical") "internal states" and the ordered sequence of its possible changes of state, so, too, *all* mental states are abstract states, definable without reference to physical or behavioral constraints. Even pain, Putnam claims (1967/1975b), "is not a brain state, in the sense of a physical-chemical state of the brain (or even the whole nervous system), but another *kind* of state entirely. I propose the hypothesis that pain, or the state of being in pain, is a functional state of a whole organism." But is Putnam right in treating the mental as *completely describable in purely abstract terms*?

It is an essential part of Putnam's functionalist theory (1967/1975b) that:

1. the laws of psychology can be derived from the functional description of actual organisms and the identification of mental states with functional states;
2. the presence of functional states actually explains the psychologically qualified behavior of organisms;
3. organisms may be "functionally isomorphic" with one another independently of differences in their physical-chemical composition (1967/1975b);
4. such organisms are of the same type or kind and fall under the same covering functional laws.

There is no question that in holding "mental states [to be], in reality, functional states of certain naturally evolved 'systems'" Putnam (1969) believes that reference to functional states provides causal explanations of mental phenomena in the same rich sense in which the "empirical identification" of heat and average kinetic energy does in the physical sciences. For Putnam, the explanatory force of functional states applies only to physically realized systems, although functional properties cannot be identified with particular physical-chemical structures (1967/1975a). Psychological laws apply, then, to physically realized systems but are formulated without reference to the presence of any physical properties.

However, there is some confusion here. First of all, even though, because they are defined as abstract states, functional states can be realized in indefinitely many alternative ways that cannot be antecedently restricted in physical respects, such states can play an explanatory role in empirical psychology *only* insofar as they are physically realized. Second, it seems impossible to understand what empirical laws of the functional sort could be, if they are not construed as governing regularities only abstracted from the set of actual physical realizations; the assumption of regularities governing independent functional phenomena only contingently linked with their realizations would commit us to a Cartesian view of abstract causes. Third, *if* psychological laws are *the laws of physically realized systems possessing functional properties* (that is, properties that are real only when physically realized but that can be abstracted from the set of all such realizations), then, contrary to Putnam, psychological properties are, based on the best empirical theory, *not* (in his sense) functional properties at all but certain complex properties—*physically realized functional properties.*

INCARNATE PROPERTIES

To use a term of art, psychological properties are not (merely) functional (that is, abstract) but *incarnate.* Incarnate properties are emergent in Feigl's sense (as specified in Chapter 2) because they cannot be subsumed under $physical_2$ terms. But to construe functional properties as both abstract *and* as being in accord with the three propositions already mentioned is to subscribe to Cartesianism (ontic dualism). The idea is that a psychological property designates a certain distinctive way in which a system functions:

1. the system must have physical properties;
2. its functioning as it does cannot be described solely in terms of its physical properties;
3. it cannot be said to function as it does except through the physical properties that it has.

The psychological property is, in this sense, both *emergent* (not reducible to the physical) and *incarnate* (linked as indissolubly emergent with respect to the physical). To ascribe psychological properties, though we deny or believe we need not consider the just-mentioned first or third attribute of a system, is to treat the psychological as abstract or in accord with ontic dualism.

We cannot, of course, set *a priori* constraints on *how* functional properties must be incarnated in order to count as psychological; that is rightly seen to be an empirical matter. Nevertheless, to treat selected systems *as* psychological (say, in examining forms of life in outer space, or even in examining nonhuman animals) is to depend on comparing the explanatory power of doing so with the psychological explanation of human behavior. Psychologically endowed systems must be incarnated in some way judged suitably similar to the incarnation of the psychological properties ascribed to our paradigms—ourselves.

There may not be any physically necessary conditions for the realization of psychological properties; but if the point of conceding that functional properties may be realized in alternative ways *is to facilitate the discovery of psychological laws,* then the extended use of psychological terms is bound to be constrained by regularities observed to hold among suitably incarnate phenomena. And that means that there *are* physical constraints on the identification of psychological properties.

Fodor (1968) presses the point most tellingly. He distinguishes between "first phase" and "second phase" psychological explanations. In the first phase, "the primary concern [of explanations] is with determining the functional character of the states and processes involved in the etiology of behavior . . . [where] the hypothesized psychological constructs are individuated primarily or solely by reference to their alleged causal consequences" (pp. 107–108). (This statement most closely corresponds to Putnam's account.) But "the second phase . . . has to do with the specification of those biochemical systems that do, in fact, exhibit the functional characteristics enumerated by phase-one theories" (p. 109). For example, a chess-playing machine may be assigned a "first phase" psychological explanation in virtue of the functional similarity between the machine's chess "moves" and those of an informed human player. But the differences between the physical processes involved in the two systems (machine and man)—that is, in producing putative chess moves—may well preclude a "second phase" psychological explanation for the machine. The concept of machine simulation is equivocal in this regard: Machines are said to "emulate" the behavior or functional abilities of other systems, notably the human—in that sense, they are (functionally) "weakly equivalent" to what they emulate; on the other hand, to count *as* psychologically endowed, they must also be able to "execute" suitable cognitive procedures in emulating what they emulate—and in that sense, they are (functionally) "strongly equivalent" (see Pylyshyn, 1980). Furthermore, apart from the distinction between weak and strong equivalence, it is entirely possible to extend the use of psychological terms—without a change of meaning (Putnam, 1975)—in such a way that the extended use (as in speaking of a robot's making calculations or decisions, in the absence of strong equivalences) will not enter into the formulation of psychophysical laws. Needless to say, there are bound to be fundamental disputes about the characterization of the intervening cognitive processes in virtue of which a system is regarded as genuinely psychologically apt. The issue will occupy us more at length in the next chapter.

Fodor invites us to ponder the question "whether or not the nervous system [or other comparable system of an organism or robot] *does* in fact contain parts *capable* of performing the alleged functions" (italics added). How, for example, could we possibly claim that a robot (Hal, say, in

Kubrick's film *2001*) or an organism from another planet actually felt pain, if we could not, in a causal sense, link its (apparently pain-manifesting) behavior with its own incarnate states and processes—thought, on the strength of a given theory, to function similarly to the way in which neural processes facilitate pain discrimination in man? To reason thus is, of course, not to deny that psychological laws may have to be formulated in terms neutral to alternative forms of incarnation. But to admit that statement is *not* to concede that psychological explanations can be provided in purely functional (abstract) terms; it is only to concede that functional uniformities are relatively indifferent to a *certain* disputable range of alternative causally effective incarnations.

The force of this adjustment comes out very clearly in speaking of the machine simulation of intelligent behavior, and hence, in confirming our objection to a radical behaviorist test for intelligence. Here, Fodor's view (1968) is entirely compelling on its face:

> . . . a machine that can do (precisely or approximately) what Smith can do, even if it is inclined to do it (only or approximately) when Smith is, might nevertheless do it in ways that are very different from the way in which Smith does it. Now, I think it is simply analytic that a correct psychological explanation of Smith's behavior is one that correctly describes the psychological processes upon which his behavior is contingent. Hence, for an adequate simulation to be an adequate explanation it must be the case *both* that the behaviors available to the machine correspond to the behaviors available to the organism and that the processes whereby the machine produces behavior simulate the processes whereby the organism does (pp. 135–136).

Fodor's point is that not only the behavior but also the psychological processes generating the behavior must be *functionally* equivalent in some suitable way. To judge effectively whether the equivalence obtains is to judge whether (say) the neurological and electronic processes *of* given systems (incarnate systems, in the idiom we have adopted) *are* functionally equivalent. To say that the equivalence is *functional* is to say that the causal explanation of the relevant behavior cannot be provided solely in physical terms. But to say that *there is* a functional equivalence is to say that the realized systems in question have similar functional properties. The causal efficacy of the psychological processes of such systems *is* the efficacy of their incarnate processes, not merely of their (abstracted) functional processes. Obviously, the internal (incarnate) processes posited as causally effective are posited by way of an inference regarding *what* functional interpretation of actual physical processes would best account for the functionally characterized behavior of a given system or organism.

This accords very closely with Ned Block's account (1978), possibly the most sustained criticism of functionalism to date. In Block's view, the chief weakness of behaviorism is "liberalism," that is, the habit of "ascribing mental properties to things that do not in fact have them"; the counterpart weakness of physicalism is "chauvinism," since it "withholds mental properties from systems that in fact have them." But it is Block's contention, also, that functionalism is typically "liberal"; in any case, "no version of functionalism [he believes] can avoid both liberalism and chauvinism." Thus construed, Putnam is simply mistaken in conflating the claim that there are no necessary (or necessary and sufficient) physical-chemical conditions for pain (or any other psychological states) with the claim that there are no physical-chemical limitations on psychological states at all. Quite correctly, Putnam argues that we cannot suppose that mere terrestrial cases establish necessary physical conditions for psychological states anywhere in the universe. Nevertheless, the paradigms of psychological phenomena are afforded, first, by ourselves and, second, on inferential grounds, by some subset of the animal world. And this situation imposes physical, biological, and behavioral conditions (*not* necessary, but theoretically pertinent conditions) on the ascription of psychological attributes. In a word, it seems preposterous to suppose that there are no neural-*like* or behavior*like* considerations in virtue of which pain may be ascribed to an alien system.

Behaviorism is bound to appear "liberal" (in Block's idiom), given the implausibility of the following thesis: "that two organisms are in the same psychological state whenever their behaviors and/or behavioral dispositions are identical"; for that thesis cannot be readily reconciled (if at all) with: (1) the fact that mental states and behavior are only contingently connected (mentalism), and (2) the possibility of causal interaction between the two (see Block & Fodor, 1972). The corresponding implausibility ("chauvinism") of physicalism suggests itself at once.

INFORMATION AND TELEOLOGY

As an alternative to physicalism and behaviorism, *functionalism* is primarily an ontological (or "linguistic") thesis that mental states are identical with functional states. Its seeming plausibility, however, is due to a confusion of issues. First of all, it is true that functional states are "logical" or abstract states and may be defined entirely by reference to machine tables (as Putnam holds) or by similar abstract schemata, and also, that such states may (given the ingenuity of machine technology, for instance) be fairly described by extending the use of psychological terms—as in speaking of a machine's calculations. But it is not true (and it certainly does not follow) that genuine psychological states may also be defined as (abstract) functional states. Second, it is true that psychologically informed behavior may be simulated in a "weakly equivalent" way (as Fodor suggests) by machines that are not themselves psychologically competent. But it is not true (and it certainly does not follow) that an adequate explanation of psychologically informed behavior can be provided either by reference to purely functional states or the (weakly equivalent) incarnate simulating states of such machines.

The confusion about the adequacy of functionalism, then, very probably rests with two issues:

1. the analysis of information, or informational properties, and the relationship between such properties and psychological properties;
2. the question whether, if an automaton may simulate a finite range of the behavior of psychologically qualified organisms (human beings, in particular), those organisms may also be construed as automata.

Putnam is responsible, in a way, for prolonging confusion on both issues. For he holds (1960) that "the various issues and puzzles that make up the traditional mind-body problem are *wholly* linguistic and logical in character: whatever few empirical 'facts' there may be in this area support one view as much as another" (italics added); also, that "everything is a Probabilistic Automaton under *some* Description (1967/1975a). But both these claims are either extremely misleading or false, and a resolution of the two issues just mentioned would go a good distance toward undermining the initial plausibility of functionalism. Here, we shall explore the first issue only.

It is extremely useful (and fashionable) to construe *functional* properties as *informational,* that is, as properties represented or modeled intensionally or linguistically and as involving feedback. Certainly, the notion Putnam borrows from cybernetics, that functional (and psychological) attributes are definable entirely in terms of machine tables, is hospitable to such a construction. In fact, Norbert Wiener (1950/1954) explicitly links cybernetics to communicated "messages" and construes "information [as] a name for the content of what is exchanged with the outer world [messages] as we adjust to it, and make our adjustment felt upon it" (p. 26). Information is what circulates in a communication system; it is abstract, distinct from its physical manifestation, and represented in alternative ways by "languages." In its now standardized sense, however, information theory is not concerned with the actual semantic component of functional "messages," but only with the statistical probabilities that any given set of signals will successfully convey information through a given communicative channel (see Shannon & Weaver, 1949).

Still, in fields as diverse as genetics and the machine simulation of intelligence, that is, in the study of what we have been calling incarnate systems, information is specifically construed in terms of the content of purported "messages," "instructions," "rules," and the like, which are linguistically modeled. For example, J. D. Watson (1970) remarks:

> DNA itself is not the direct template [that is, "the macromolecular mold for the synthesis of another macromolecule"] that orders amino sequences. Instead, the genetic information of DNA is transferred to another class of molecules, which then serve as the protein templates. These intermediate templates are molecules of ribonucleic acid (RNA), large polymeric molecules chemically very similar to DNA.

The relation specified is termed "the central dogma," that is, the thesis that "RNA sequences are never copied on protein templates; likewise, RNA never acts as a template for DNA" (pp. 330–331). Other specimen remarks randomly drawn from contemporary genetics would include many like the following (Stebbins, 1972; cf. Monod, 1970/1971):

> One group of geneticists and biochemists have assumed that DNA, which is the universal basis of genetic information in cellular organisms today, has always been the only kind of molecule to play this role. Based upon this assumption, they have postulated that life began when the first DNA molecule was constructed which could transmit functionally significant genetic information.

Correspondingly, in the development of programs of artificial intelligence (AI), we readily find remarks of the following sort (Fahlman, 1979):

> The human mind can do many remarkable things. Of these, perhaps the most remarkable is the mind's ability to store a huge quantity and variety of knowledge about its world, and to locate and retrieve whatever it needs from this storehouse at the proper time. . . . If we are ever to create an artificial intelligence with human-like abilities, we will have to endow it with a comparable knowledge-handling facility. . . . The system presented here consists of two more-or-less independent parts. First, there is the system's parallel network memory scheme. Knowledge is stored as a pattern of interconnections of very simple parallel processing elements. . . . The second, more traditional part of the knowledge-based system is a vocabulary of conventions and processing algorithms—in some sense, a language—for representing various kinds of knowledge as nodes and links in the network (pp. 1–2; cf. Boden, 1977; Feigenbaum & Feldman, 1963; Minsky, 1968; Winograd, 1972/1976).

We must be careful, of course. The informational or functional idiom is sometimes introduced heuristically—where physicalism or eliminative materialism is thought adequate but inconvenient in terms of predictive and similar concerns (see Feigl, 1958/1967; Sellars, 1963). It is precisely in this sense that the question arises whether what is "encoded" in DNA is to be construed realistically or heuristically. The issue is empirical, and the answer is not in. But the realist thesis, that there *is* a code incarnate in DNA, entails that biology is emergent (in Feigl's sense) relative to physics, and that the genetic explanation of biological phenomena requires the introduction of physically irreducible attributes from which formal informational features may be *abstracted*.

Functional attributes may be empirically specified at whatever level of abstraction proves fruitful; that is, they appear, where required, in the *analysis* of complex phenomena. But where they are thought to bear on the *causal* explanation of those phenomena they must (on pain of dualism) count as emergent features of elements actually capable of playing a causal role. At best, functional analyses may be thought of as elliptical accounts of incarnate systems.

A question arises, however, about the replacement or elimination of functional attributes—hence, of incarnate attributes. Charles Taylor (1964) has posed the issue in a particularly perspicuous way—construing functional attributes *teleologically*: "To offer a teleological explanation of some event or class of events, e.g., the behavior of some being, is, then, to account for it by laws in terms of which an event's occurring is held to be dependent on that event's being required for some end" (p. 9). The feature of "purposiveness" in such a system (in Taylor's view) is:

1. "not a separable feature [of any element or elements within a given system], but a property of the whole system" (p. 10) sufficient (under the appropriate circumstances) for the occurrence of the event in question;
2. not, as such, necessarily a psychological or cognitively qualified feature;
3. not expressible in terms of (what Taylor calls) laws of the "atomistic" sort.

Teleological laws, therefore, are taken to be *sui generis.* They fail to meet certain critical conditions, and for that reason, challenge (if conceded) the methodological objectives of the unity of science program—that is, the objective of demonstrating that explanation in the physical and behavioral sciences is systematically uniform and physicalistic. They do satisfy the (atomistic) constraint that "the antecedent and the consequent [of some putative law] must be separately identifiable" (and may occur independently of one another). But they cannot meet the further requirement (said to be a defining feature of atomistic laws) that "the two terms which are linked in a law . . . be identified separately from *any* law in which [either] may figure, i.e., that it not be a condition for the identification of any term that it be linked to any other" (p. 11). Teleological laws are clearly informational laws, that is, laws involving functional attributes, applied holistically to incarnate systems. In order to eliminate functional attributes in the contexts in which such teleological laws are said to obtain, it would be necessary: (1) to replace the functional (teleological) characterization of the elements of a given system "atomistically," in effect, in some way that did not entail reference to the alleged teleological system; and (2) to replace the teleological laws themselves with some suitable set of atomistic laws ranging over the same phenomena, even if no single such law would or could exhibit the range of the original teleological law (see Davidson, 1970; Fodor, 1975). It might be supposed, for instance, that homeostatic phenomena would lend themselves to such a reduction, but the issue, of course, is an empirical one.

The important question to ask is not merely whether psychological or biological systems may be explained in nonfunctional or noninformational terms; one must also ask whether the difference between the psychological and the nonpsychological (or the cognitive and noncognitive) is itself an informational distinction of an empirically pertinent sort. Certainly, at the level of paradigmatic self-ascriptions of psychological states—that is, at the level of linguistically informed (human) psychological states—abilities are manifested that do not appear at the level of languageless animals or at the level of subsensory systems (DNA). But if informational feedback is said to be represented and to provide the data for computation within a given system—in the way, say, in which Wiener and Watson speak—there may not be any empirical difference of importance to be marked by the cognitive/noncognitive distinction; although graded and qualitative differences within the range of feedback phenomena may well remain crucial at the explanatory level. If psychological systems are construed in terms of the flow of information, then informational feedback is essential. It may well be unavoidable—say, at the level of very low animal life—to introduce a teleological (or an informational) schema of explanation. There, however, either feedback does not play a central role (imagine that animal responses to stimuli are too rigid, too "hardwired," for that) or else informational feedback is itself introduced only heuristically (as in explaining a plant's search for nutrients).

Here, again, Taylor's account is instructive. For Taylor (1964) remarks that "something more than teleological explanation is required for us to use the notion of action, and . . . the notion of desire as well" (and similar psychologically qualified notions) (p. 55). It is certainly possible that the DNA molecule *has* informational properties, in virtue of which it *does* function teleologically. This in itself does not entail that the DNA molecule *has* psychological capacities (see Dawkins, 1976). The difference between the biological and the psychological need not be construed, therefore, in terms of the physical reducibility of the first alone; it may be construed more aptly in terms of the specific nature and ("second phase") complexity of the functional (or informational or teleological) properties of the two sorts of system—specifically, in terms of feedback.

CONSCIOUSNESS AND COGNITION

At the level of human behavior, there can be no serious conceptual difficulty about the ascrib*ability* of psychological states. The reason is simply that: (1) humans, exclusively, are able to report their mental states; (2) given (1), they provide the paradigms of (having or possessing) mental states; and (3) given (1) and (2), the intentional nature of mental states is best (perhaps inescapably) modeled on the propositional structure of language. The paradigms of psychological states, therefore, are the cognitively informed, conscious molar states of humans that humans can report—for instance, states conveyed by such statements as *I saw that she nudged her husband; I believe that Cairo is the capital of Egypt. If* (as Putnam, 1978, seems to think possible in principle, though not perhaps realizable within any manageable future) a machine program could be imposed on the totality of human behavior, then, we could, from a knowledge of such a program, read off from particular physical and behavioral manifestations the propositional content of corresponding mental states. Lacking such a program, we are (at best) reduced to *ascribing* such content to given neurophysiological states, on empirically reasonable grounds, in a way, however, that cannot be independently discovered or checked (see Dennett, 1969).

The idea of modeling mental states linguistically or propositionally is controversial, of course. We cannot provide a full account of the matter here. But *if*, as we have already argued, linguistic phenomena are real and physically irreducible, then the paradigms of psychological states at least—in accord with statements (1) and (2), above—must be linguistically modeled, that is, irreducibly characterized in terms of the rich intensional structures of the natural languages in which they are expressed. Beyond this, statement (3) poses the possibility that *all* mental states, those among humans that are not linguistically expressed as well as those among nonlinguistically apt animals, are characterized in ways that depend conceptually on the model appropriate to characterizing the paradigms.

Even D. M. Armstrong (1973), who firmly believes that "the mind can be (contingently) identified with the brain," holds that beliefs, which he treats as intentionally qualified "maps [representations] of the world in the light of which we are prepared to act," are "literally" maps "in the believer's head" (pp. 3–4). Armstrong has noticeable difficulty in reducing incarnate states to purely physical states. He concedes that beliefs "have the unique, irreducible characteristic of *intentionality*. It is in virtue of this that belief-states are self-directed" (p. 54). Nevertheless, Armstrong wishes to concede the irreducibility of intentionality (the *sine qua non* of the "self-directed" nature of mental states), to neutralize that concession in physicalist terms, *and* to eliminate the propositional characterization of the content of mental states. His attempt may well be the most sustained and informed effort of this sort to date. He offers the following resolution: "My contention is that [simple concepts, the putative constituents of our beliefs] are certain sorts of selective capacity towards things that fall under the concept in question. And this . . . constitutes their *self-directedness*" (p. 60). We have, here, an extraordinarily straightforward thesis: Simple concepts "must be" selective capacities; *qua* simple, "they are nothing but such selective capacities"; *qua* capacities (*contra* behaviorism), they "must be conceived of as *states* of the thing that has the capacity" (p. 60).

The difficulty of Armstrong's proposal concerns how the capacities in question can be empirically known to be controlled *by the concepts in question* and not by any other. Of course, as Armstrong acknowledges, concepts may be intensionally distinct (distinct in meaning) even if coextensive in their range of application—for instance, concepts like *being a creature with a heart* and *being a creature with a kidney*. Armstrong says, for example:

> A's concept of red is a *second-order* capacity—a capacity to acquire the capacity to react towards the red object when the latter acts upon A's mind . . . the *first-order* capacity is rather to be identified with a certain elementary type of *belief* (p. 61).
>
> The concept of red is the concept of *red* because the red object that activates this concept (by producing an appropriate "map" of the object involving the Idea of red) has this effect in *virtue of the object's redness*. . . . And that is the criterion for calling it the concept of red (p. 69).

The obvious trouble is that although the concept thus activated is the concept of red, we must face the fact that the requisite beliefs cannot be characterized solely in terms of the selective capacities identified independently of the concepts in question; they can be identified only in terms of selective capacities-to-respond-to-things-*in-virtue-of-certain-concepts-activated-by-the-appropriate-properties-of-such-things*. Here, then, the operative concepts are themselves identified by means of the same linguistic modeling involved in specifying the propositional content of beliefs. There simply is no empirical way in which Armstrong's proposal can escape circularity. Hence, there are very strong grounds for supposing that the linguistic modeling of the content of mental states is unavoidable.

Our conclusion bears directly and powerfully on the characterization of the mental states of animals that lack language. For if they may be ascribed mental states although they lack language (see Davidson, 1975; Malcolm, 1973; Premack, 1976; Sibley, 1971; Terrace, 1980; Vendler, 1972), animal psychology cannot fail to be anthropomorphized, in the precise sense that the ascription of mental states must be *modeled* linguistically. Alternatively put, if animals *have* (real) mental states, *we* cannot characterize them except *heuristically*, that is, by the use of the linguistic model that serves our paradigm cases. They *have* mental states, and mental states are (in Armstrong's sense) "self-directed," intentional. Such states, *ex hypothesi*, are real; but although they lack the distinction (and complexities) of human states, *we* cannot specify them except in terms of how we model our own (reflexive) mental states, that is, propositionally.

The intensional puzzles concerning human language—nonsynonymy with respect to coextensive expressions, so-called opaque contexts of reference, and the rest—*simply do not arise in the context of animal psychology*. We *treat* animals as capable of making one discrimination rather than another, which, again, we model by reference to human concepts. But conceding this much, we never suppose that (lacking language) an animal is ever confronted with specifically intensional puzzles. For instance, if a dog may be said to see *that its master is at the door,* there need be no sense in which we are bound to consider, assuming that the dog's master = the president of the First National Bank, that the dog sees *that the president of the First National Bank is at the door.* The dog lacks the discriminative ability that the concept of bank president heuristically captures; and, in any case, it lacks the ability to discriminate intensional distinctions.

To some extent, something very similar obtains even in the *human* context, as in ascribing thoughts in nonverbal contexts (playing tennis, for instance) or in inferring how one "must" have arrived at a certain "decision" judged by one's behavior. Here, we begin to see the inevitably idealized aspect of imputing mental states in accordance with an empirically reasonable model of rational behavior—without, by the way, any point-by-point reference to neurophysiological states (see Harman, 1973). By a related extension, the biological use of functional characterizations is similarly parasitic on linguistic reporting. This accounts for the anthropomorphized idiom ("the selfish gene," for instance) even at the level of DNA (see Dawkins, 1976). These linkages suggest the possibility of a unified picture of a number of sciences systematically organized in terms of the central role of linguistically informed psychological states—though not the possibility of restoring the unity of science program. Thus, machines and genes may be characterized functionally or informationally in ways that are at least "weakly" equivalent to the psychological, because their molar "behavior" is suitably analogous to the psychological. They remain functionally dissimilar in the "strong" sense, however, that the internal processes causally responsible for such "behavior" fail to exhibit the requisite incarnate resemblances.

It needs to be stressed that as with all psychological concepts, *consciousness* is paradigmatically ascribed (self-ascribed) among human beings. It cannot, therefore, be construed solely as a theoretical notion, that is, as a notion first introduced at the level of explanation—only subsequently assigned a descriptive role.

Cognition presupposes consciousness, not in the sense that all instances of knowledge are instances of conscious knowledge (empirical evidence runs against that thesis) but in the sense that ascriptions of unconscious psychological states presuppose systems to which conscious psychological states may first be ascribed. This accounts at least for the plausibility of the Freudian unconscious. Furthermore, consciousness is paradigmatically ascribed to *molar* agents—persons and their animal counterparts—not (or at least not initially) to any submolar parts (see Dennett, 1969; Margolis, 1978a), certainly not to the brain, the cerebral hemispheres, or other parts of the brain without a suitable reductive argument (cf. Bogen, 1969a, 1969b; Gazzaniga, 1979). On the strength of what has already been said, consciousness should be construed in incarnate terms. It is difficult to see, also, how the "conscious" can fail to be construed in terms that include the sentient and phenomenal (images, sensations, feelings, and the like). These would be ignored by functionalism (see Block & Fodor, 1972). Similarly, even at the molar level, consciousness may on occasion be functionally compartmentalized, as the evidence of remembering and forgetting, multiple personality, amnesia, parapraxes, habituated behavior, neurosis and psychosis, hypnosis, commissurotomy, and the like confirm (see Hilgard, 1974).

Armstrong (1968) maintains that "the concept of a mental state is primarily the concept of *a state of the person apt for bringing about a certain sort of behavior*. Sacrificing all accuracy for brevity, we can say that, although mind is not behavior, it is the *cause* of behavior" (p. 82). This is an ingenious but quite misleading notion. Though it concedes a causal role to the mental, it fails to identify the mental as a state of a certain particular kind that may enter, *contingently,* into the causal relations intended. It defines the mental functionally *by* defining it as whatever occupies a certain causal role. It also construes the mental in a peculiarly abstract way, without regard to its phenomenal aspects. (The apparent restriction to persons Armstrong amends elsewhere.) But Armstrong goes on to admit that "consciousness is something more than the occurrence of an inner state apt for the production of certain sorts of behavior"; for, "unlike the gene, the mind is not a mere theoretical concept. In our own case, at least, we have a direct awareness of mental states" (p. 93). Nevertheless, the concession comes to no more than this: "consciousness is no more than *awareness* (perception) of inner mental states by the person whose states they are"; it "is simply a further mental state, a state 'directed' towards the original inner states . . . an inner state apt [once again] for the production of certain behavior." Since he is committed to a form of central-state materialism, Armstrong maintains as well that in consciousness, "one part of the brain scans another part of the brain" (p. 94).

In itself, this raises no new problems: We have, in Chapter 2, already examined the difficulties of the identity theory. But a careful reading of Armstrong's account of *perception,* which he takes to be equivalent to *awareness* (cf. Armstrong, 1962, 1973), conclusively shows that it is to be treated in precisely the same way as any other general mental state. Hence, it need not be conscious. *When* it is conscious, it is such merely in virtue of being "directed" to another mental state (that is, the "flow of information" from another mental state). In Armstrong's view, even unconscious states "directed" to further states are fully conscious: This is surely a *reductio ad absurdum.*

Armstrong does succeed, nevertheless, in linking ascriptions of consciousness to a model of rationality, though he does not explicitly develop the connection (see Davidson, 1970; Taylor, 1964). This is important, because although consciousness cannot (in the human context) be introduced solely as a theoretical concept, its use entails the adoption of a certain holistic, species-specific model of the normal connection among such phenomena as desire, belief, intention, and action—adjusted empirically to the different species—in virtue of which certain linkages are expected to hold. For example, in general, one cannot be said to intend to do what one believes is already done or is impossible to do (see Meiland, 1970). In this regard, *consciousness* is the generic feature of the states of desire, perception, belief, want, motive, and intention relative to the kind of behavior that distinguishes the life of the members of one species from that of another. The model of the connections among such states specifies the form of "rationality" of each species capable of a mental life: The "rationality" of the great carnivores, for instance, can hardly be the same as that of their prey.

Consciousness, therefore, seems best reserved for molar agents, but the idea has been contested (in a way that bears decisively on the topics of the next chapter). Daniel Dennett (1969), for instance, proposes to replace

> the ordinary personal level term "aware" by two terms that still take persons (or whole systems as subjects, but [that] have sub-personal criteria: (1) A is $aware_1$ that *p* at time *t* if and only if *p* is the content of the input state of A's 'speech center' at time *t*; (2) A is $aware_2$ that *p* at time *t* if and only if *p* is the content of an internal event in A at time *t* that is effective in directing current behavior (pp. 118–119).

Animals are (said to be) only $aware_2$; persons may be $aware_1$ and $aware_2$. The trouble is that even in Dennett's view—certainly on independent grounds—the (intentional) content of any relevant "input state" or "internal event" can only be *assigned* to the subpersonal agent (the homunculus) on the basis of the function of that part or agent *in* the functioning of the original molar agent itself. Homunculi simply *have* no function except as factors within, or as causally facilitating, the functioning *of* some molar system. So the best that Dennett could hope for here is that *whatever* would count as the marks of molar consciousness could be suitably factored as the distributed contribution of a set of homuncular agents; but that is to say that homuncular contributions could *never* serve independently as the *criteria* of consciousness or awareness.

Two quite distinct issues, then, are linked by the concept of consciousness: (1) that of ascribing psychological attributes to molar or submolar agents, and (2) that of construing psychological attributes as functional or incarnate. It is the intentionality of mental states that settles both issues. For the assignment of intentional functions to submolar agents makes their characterization conceptually dependent on ascriptions to molar agents; and the causal efficacy of mental states obliges us to construe such states as incarnated rather than in dualistic terms. Once this is conceded, we cannot fail to see that functionalist accounts of mental states tend to ignore or impoverish the fully biological and cultural settings within which at least human existence flourishes. The question remains whether an adequate philosophy of psychology requires conceptual resources beyond the infrapsychological, beyond whatever may be taken to be internal to the life and functioning of individual human organisms. In particular, the question arises whether the analysis of psychological phenomena at the human level (that is, paradigmatically) requires the provision of social and historical processes that cannot themselves be adequately characterized solely in psychologically internalized terms. Linguistic behavior, for instance, is paradigmatically manifested by psychologically apt creatures and provides, in turn, the paradigms of the psychological. But language itself is a highly structured network of practices that can hardly be mastered or internalized completely by each and every linguistically apt agent. If so, then the social and historically changing aspects of language cannot be accounted for solely in terms of relations among an aggregate of psychologically and linguistically apt agents; and yet, the explanation of their own behavior and mental states must depend conceptually on such psychologically irreducible social and historical factors. Furthermore, what is true of language in this respect is bound to be true as well of the more general institutions and practices of human culture. In short, we must ask ourselves what the conceptual and methodological connection is between psychology and the social or so-called human sciences. To do so, however, is to reject functionalism.

CHAPTER FIVE

Cognitivism

COGNITIVISM AND THE SCIENCE OF PSYCHOLOGY

We have come to a point in our reflections about the analysis of psychological states in which it is already clear that our chief findings seriously affect the prospects of psychology as a science or (alternatively) the prospects of characterizing science uniformly for physics and psychology. The matter is quite complicated and needs to be sorted carefully. In effect, three distinct features of our discourse about psychological states are bound to challenge certain canonical views of the nature of science (views we have already collected, in Chapter 2, as the unity of science program). These include: (1) *the holism of the mental;* (2) *the irreducibility of the intentional and the intensional;* and (3) *the causal efficacy of mental states.* These are surely the most strategic distinctions we have broached thus far. Admittedly, they are all controversial, and each (as we have seen) has been strenuously opposed. Of the three, the first has perhaps been somewhat slighted in the preceding chapters; the vindication of the second rests with the weakness or indefensibility of reductive programs of the materialist, behaviorist, and functionalist varieties; and the third favors the emergence of incarnate properties and the avoidance of all forms of ontic dualism. They are, however, interconnected distinctions and, taken together, bear in a powerful way on the theory of psychology as a science.

For example, if, as we have already seen, linguistic phenomena cannot be *excluded* from the domain of empirical psychology (*contra* Sellars, 1963) simply because human beings are actually capable of speech, then, against an extremely influential thesis advanced by Donald Davidson (1970), the physical sciences *cannot* form "a comprehensive closed theory" whose laws are physically "homonomic" (that is, whose laws are expressed or expressible in a vocabulary limited, say, to physical$_2$ terms). Davidson claims that "the mental does not . . . constitute a closed system"—mental phenomena may, after all, interact with physical phenomena that cannot be characterized in mental terms. Nevertheless, "it is [he insists] a feature of physical reality that physical change can be explained by laws that connect it with other changes and conditions physically described." His claim holds *only if* some relevant form of reduction obtains; for *if* the mental can interact with the physical, then Davidson must explain how causal connections *affecting the physical* can be accounted for in exclusively physical terms. But if, as we have argued, causal interaction holds, *and* the mental is not reducible to the physical, then the physical sciences themselves *can no longer be said to form "a closed system"* for all relevant phenomena. The relevant closed system would have to be an incarnate system—a psychological or social or cultural system of some sort. One sees, therefore, the profound allure of the various sorts of reductive theories we have canvassed *and* their conceptual link to a certain scientific methodology now rendered seriously—perhaps irrevocably—vulnerable.

The scientific prospects of psychology become even more puzzling if we bear in mind that an essential part of Davidson's motivation for insisting on the "homonomic" nature of physical science (correspondingly, for insisting on what he calls his "anomalous monism"—the token but not type identity of mental and physical phenomena—that is, the nonlawlike connection between the mental and the physical) rests, precisely, with the danger *that even some purely physical phenomena would not, on the admission of psychological emergence, be able to be subsumed under universal causal laws.* This would follow, for Davidson, because he is persuaded of the truth of the holism of the mental; for this distinction entails the consequence that phenomena cannot, insofar as they are characterized in mental terms, be shown to fall under lawlike regularities. Hence, *if* mental discourse is used holistically, and *if* causal interaction is conceded, then the homonomic nature of science (ultimately, of physical science) cannot be assured unless some form of physicalist reduction is also assured. But this is just what we have found to be uncertain—or impossible. According to Davidson (1970):

> We know too much about thought and behavior to trust exact and universal statements linking them. Beliefs and desires issue in behavior only as modified and mediated by further beliefs and desires, attitudes, and attendings, without end. Clearly this holism of the mental realm is a clue both to the autonomy and to the anomalous character of the mental . . . nomological slack between the mental and the physical is essential as long as we conceive of man as a rational animal.

By *holism,* then, we may understand an essential constraint on mental or psychological ascriptions—in accord with which all particular ascriptions conceptually depend on other such ascriptions, no limit to such dependencies can in principle be provided, all are linked to one another in terms of a species-specific model of rationality, and (therefore) mental ascriptions cannot as such be treated extensionally.

If, therefore, the holism of the mental is confirmed, *and* the various reductive programs we have considered prove untenable, the extensionalist undertaking we have been tracking in so many different ways will be seen to have obscured in a most remarkable way the fact that the explanation of human behavior cannot, for conceptual reasons, be freed from the peculiarly *historical, culturally qualified, linguistically informed, rationally interconnected* causal forces that groom the actual psychological abilities of human agents. Empirical psychology would then belong to the same system of "human studies" of which sociology and anthropology form distinct parts often thought incapable of satisfying the conditions of a genuine science. But even if one held (against Davidson's view) that there could be such laws, psychophysical laws would entail the consequence that the physical was not homonomic with respect to psychological and cultural phenomena *and,* even more radically, that such laws would not have the same logical properties as physical laws.

Under the circumstances, the least extreme adjustments designed to accommodate the scientific status of psychology would (1) concede that the physical was not homonomic, that some sort of functional or incarnate causal laws obtained at the level of psychological emergence; and (2) reinterpret the functioning of molar agents (persons and their animal and machine counterparts) in ways that would obviate the methodological impact of holism. This would not in itself insure the conventional standing of psychology as a science; but it might permit a useful enlargement of the concept of science itself. The issue, of course, becomes most pressing just at the point at which human agents behave in their most distinctive way—linguistically or in accord with culturally rich practices (composing and playing music, for instance). Here, the explanation of the cognitive powers of molar agents becomes decisive, the central concern of what has come to be called *cognitive science*—whether construed biologically, ethologically, informationally or semiotically—in terms of linguistic competence or artificial intelligence or machine simulation—psychologically, or culturally. All efforts, then, to explain cognitive powers in accordance with the two adjustments just mentioned may be collected as varieties of *cognitivism*—which is the latest and most resilient phase of modern attempts to construe psychology as a science.

A salient distinction provides a useful economy: Psychology after all, is bifurcated; we cannot deny that there must be psychological processes explicable solely in terms that include the biological and exclude whatever pertains to acquiring the skills and habits of a particular human culture. For example, there is every reason to believe that the psychotropic drugs exhibit causal uniformities *both* relatively independent of cultural factors and subject to some extent to the effects of particular cultural variables (see Valzelli, 1973). Also, as in the famous "visual cliff" phenomenon among infants (see E. J. Gibson & R. D. Walk, 1960) and (at least to some extent) in what appears to be the genetically programmed responsiveness of animals within their ecological niches (see Gibson, 1979), there is good reason to think that there are biologically regular perceptual and affective processes already in place before cultural grooming that cannot be altogether overridden or radically modified (see Segall, 1966). It is understandable, therefore—particularly since the demarcation between the biological and the cultural becomes increasingly problematic as perceptual, linguistic, and ratiocinative capacities are assigned a genetic component—to attempt to meet methodological constraints like these distinctions, just given, by treating cultural regularities as somehow generated biologically.

In rather different, quite influential ways—but still within the cognitivist spirit—this is precisely what is attempted by J. J. Gibson (1966); Jean Piaget (1979/1980); and Noam Chomsky (1980). In Chomsky's view, for instance, at least an essential part of language—the innate knowledge of grammar—*is* genetically determined; its culturally variable features are said to be caused by the interaction between genetic and environmental factors, by the production of phenotypic variations of an underlying genotype. Hence, Chomsky treats

> the theory of particular and universal grammar . . . as that aspect of theoretical psychology . . . primarily concerned with the genetically determined program that specifies the range of possible grammars for human languages and the particular realizations of this schematism that arise under given conditions (p. 202).

Chomsky's theory constitutes an extreme cognitivist resolution of the scientific status of psychology. In one respect at least, it is decidedly more radical than Freud's theory of the unconscious, for in Chomsky's view, in "knowing" or "cognizing . . . the grammar that constitutes the current state of our language faculty and the rules of this system as well as the principles that govern their operation," we cognize what "may be and in the interesting cases is inaccessible to consciousness" (pp. 69–70). It is normally not possible, then, for a human agent to recover by introspective means (as, in psychoanalysis, one tries to do with repressed material) the deep grammatical rules of language; or for others spontaneously to provide such rules merely by observing the other's behavior. Chomsky, therefore, uses a cognitive vocabulary to specify human powers that "have the structure and character of knowledge," but (1) are not consciously accessible, (2) are operative at some cognitively relevant infrapsychological level, and (3) are genetically determined. This doctrine constitutes a form of cognitivism that is variously termed *innatism, nativism,* or (contemporary) *rationalism* (Chomsky, 1966). It is, of course, Chomsky's inference to the best explanation of the facts about language acquisition and use that leads him to believe that our competence must be cognitively innate.

Cognitivism, however, need not be committed to innatism, although *every* cognitive psychology must admit *some* innate structuring of the mind. Even John Locke implicitly admits a structured sensorium, within the context of his empiricism and his notorious doctrine of the *tabula rasa;* Locke himself does not provide (nor does anyone else) "a non-nativist theory of where [its] primitive features come from" (Fodor, 1979/1980; see Piaget, 1968/1970). In this sense, in current terms, psychological powers cannot fail to be genetically (or analogously) grounded: The very idea of *acquiring* a language or perceptual skill or the like would make no sense unless a suitably structured system were postulated, capable over an interval of time of manifesting some form of growth, learning, or programming (or combination of these) constituting such acquisition. Hence, innatism *of some sort* is generally admitted to be unavoidable. The question remains, however, how extensive it must be, and whether, in particular, linguistic ability must be accounted for in terms of innate *linguistic* competence (Chomsky's thesis). It is not even clear whether or how the thesis of innate linguistic competence *can* be treated as an explicitly empirical issue, and Chomsky himself retreats from the direct behavioral confirmation of innate competence (see Chomsky, 1957). These qualifications show that we need to distinguish among:

1. the essential explanatory program of all forms of cognitivism;
2. the varieties of cognitivism, particularly innatist and noninnatist versions;
3. noncognitivist theories of cognition—or of aspects of cognition—that concede an initial, innately structured system capable of realizing particular cognitive powers.

To date, perhaps the briefest and most balanced account of (the new) cognitivism has been provided by John Haugeland (1978). In Haugeland's terms:

> The fundamental idea of cognitive psychology [is]: intelligent behavior is to be explained by appeal to internal "cognitive processes"—meaning, essentially, processes interpretable as working out a rationale. Cognitivism, then, can be summed up in a slogan: the mind is to be understood as an IPS [*information processing system*]."

It is reasonably clear, both on independent grounds and in accord with Haugeland's own intention (1979), that information processing systems (conceived either in functional or incarnate terms) apply to a range of biological, electronic, and similar domains that include much more than the merely psychological (see Minsky, 1968; Newell & Simon, 1972). The thesis requires, therefore, some clarification of such notions as *cognitive, intelligent, rational, conscious,* and *mental,* in virtue of which the science of psychology may be taken to be a part—very probably the most complex part—of a comprehensive science of information processing. So far, this much accords rather nicely with our attempt to demonstrate the conceptual dependence of accounts of *non*psychological information processing on paradigm accounts of psychological phenomena.

One essential caveat arises, however. "Information" or "information processing" is equivocal in Haugeland's context. Sometimes, "information" signifies what are specifically *cognitive* phenomena, namely, phenomena characterized in terms of the real intentional or semantic content of *certain* systems, states, and processes. And sometimes "information" signifies only what is viewed (in so-called information theory) as effecting or being able to effect a reduction in the uncertainty, or an increase in the probability, of a given event; in the latter sense, any system may be viewed as an "information channel" if its output may be taken as a reliable indicator of its input without regard to its "message" (see Shannon, 1948). It hardly follows that any and all causal systems behave cognitively, in the former sense. The distinction is already adumbrated in Putnam's well-known remark (1967/1975b): "Everything is a Probabilistic Automaton under *some* Description." For if that statement be granted, then merely to provide a machine simulation or description of *any* system is hardly to characterize or to explain it in genuine cognitive terms. The same equivocation was noted earlier in discussing the Turing test of intelligence (see Dreyfus, 1972/1979; Searle, 1980). John McCarthy (1979) similarly equivocates when he offers the extreme view that "Machines as simple as thermostats can be said to have beliefs, and having beliefs seems to be a characteristic of most machines capable of problem solving performance." In much the same spirit, Allen Newell and Herbert Simon (1972) claim that "A physical symbol system [that obeys the laws of physics] has the necessary and sufficient means for general intelligent actions" (that is, "has [as such] the same scope of intelligence as we see in human actions").

We must be frank to admit that we have not explicitly characterized the "cognitive." Broadly speaking, we could do so in a way that paralleled rather closely our use of "mental" and "psychological"; that is, we could first introduce human paradigms and then argue that the extension of the term to nonhuman agents (animals and machines) was conceptually dependent on the model suited to those paradigms. This would provide a flexible enough idiom for addressing a very large range of the puzzles about cognition, for instance, those relating to conditions of species-specific rationality (Davidson, 1970) and those bearing on the psychologically irreducible social and historical features of language and culture that affect our ascriptions of knowledge to particular agents. But more than this, it is normally admitted that a state of knowledge cannot be adequately characterized infrapsychologically, for the simple reason that knowledge entails the satisfaction of a complex condition that cannot itself be construed psychologically—the condition of truth (that what one is alleged to know is actually the case) and one's relationship to the events of the world suitably linking one's mental states and one's supposed acquisition of the truth (see Chisholm, 1966/1976). This is a most controversial matter, of course. But for our own purposes it may be sufficient merely to have taken note of the complication, once we grant that the paradigms of human cognition are familiar enough and that our concern is properly limited to the psychological features of cognition. Effectively, this is precisely what the cognitivists themselves have done.

Possibly the two best known (but opposed) advocates of cognitivism in the Anglo-American philosophical literature are Jerry Fodor and Daniel Dennett. Fodor (1975) is, in effect, in accord with Haugeland, except that restricting cognitive psychology to explaining the "propositional attitudes of organisms," Fodor insists (as Haugeland does not) that the relevant theories do so "by providing, for each propositional attitude, nomologically necessary and sufficient conditions in terms of computational relations between the organism and formulae of the internal representational system" that Fodor claims every cognitive system possesses (p. 77). It should be said at once that this is an extraordinarily strong claim, which Fodor does not actually pursue in an empirically detailed way. But it is clear that the intent of Fodor's thesis is, at the very least, to offset the intensional complications of the holism of the mental that Davidson concedes. In this way, Fodor hopes to bring the new cognitivism into accord, once again, with the objectives of an extensionalist view of science.

Dennett (1978b) also concurs with Haugeland but presses a more radical thesis:

> Every cognitivist theory currently defended or envisaged, functionalist or not, is a theory of the sub-personal level. It is not at all clear to me, indeed, how a psychological theory—as distinct from a philosophical theory—could fail to be a sub-personal theory. . . . the personal level "theory" of persons is not a psychological theory.

Elsewhere (1977/1978) Dennett says (criticizing Fodor):

> Any psychology with undischarged homunculi [that is, subpersonal or submolar "agents" (homunculi) for whom "internal representations" function as such, and who are not theoretically replaced (discharged) by "agents" described in purely physical terms, without reference to representations] is doomed to circularity or infinite regress, hence psychology is impossible.

"Personal level" discourse admits the molar agency of what we normally take to be human persons. *Homunculi,* or subpersonal or submolar agents, are personlike agents not identical with persons, functioning—possibly at particular nodes in a neural network—in ways that are initially described in the intentional idiom usually reserved for persons. Dennett believes that, in principle, whatever of psychological significance is normally attributed to persons at the "personal level" may, by analysis, be distributively attributed to an aggregate of homunculi.

The conflict between Fodor and Dennett is important. Fodor attempts to develop a cognitivist account in which "personal level" functions are *not* eliminated in favor of the subpersonal (*molar cognitivism*), even if (in accord with Chomsky's orientation, which Fodor at least initially accepts) "computational relations" between the organism and internal representational system are not consciously accessible to the organism; also, Fodor clearly believes (*contra* Davidson) that strict laws obtain at the level of psychological explanation. Dennett, on the other hand, holds that personal level explanations are simply not proper explanations in the science of psychology; hence, that in principle personal level agents *and* subpersonal homunculi (introduced by way of analyzing personal level agents) must be "discharged" (eliminated or suitably replaced), or else the intended science is "doomed to circularity or infinite regress" (*homuncular cognitivism*). Both theories are noticeably extreme: Fodor preserves molar agents but attempts to account for their capacity to think, in terms of an explicitly Platonistic version of innatism; Dennett replaces molar agents with homunculi and "discharges" the latter, reverting in a roundabout way to a form of reductive materialism. Dennett's cognitivism, then, involves an homuncular *replacement* of molar functioning; and Fodor's cognitivism (and Chomsky's, and Freud's, for that matter), an *interaction* between distinct subpowers of molar functioning itself.

HOMUNCULAR COGNITIVISM

Consider, now, Dennett's homuncular account. Dennett (1978a) favors (quite reasonably) a "top-down" rather than a "bottom-up" strategy in psychology, that is, a

> . . . strategy that begins with a more abstract decomposition of the highest levels of psychological organization, and hopes to analyze these into more and more detailed smaller systems or processes until finally one arrives at elements familiar to the biologists [as opposed to a] . . . strategy [for example, "stimulus-response behaviorism" and what may be called "neuron signal physiological psychology"] that starts with some basic and well-defined unit or theoretical atom for psychology, and builds these atoms into molecules and larger aggregates that can account for the complex phenomena we all observe.

Both the empirical complexity of the neurological and the conceptual constraints imposed by reference to the intentional (particularly, the linguistic) tend to diminish, if not to discount altogether, the promise of the bottom-up strategy. *If,* in fact, the intentional and the linguistic are psychologically real and irreducible (emergent), then the bottom-up strategy must be inherently inadequate. The top-down strategy accommodates these complexities initially; although it remains an open question whether what appears emergent at the molar level can be "decomposed" into simpler elements. Dennett himself apparently believes that we can "decompose" the "highest levels of psychological organization" in terms of biological "elements." So the choice is a matter of technical convenience for him. The AI modeling of human performance is (Dennett believes) an especially promising version of the top-down strategy committed to answering the question "How is knowledge possible?" (see Moore & Newell, 1974; Pylyshyn, 1978). In any case, the efforts of the reductionists (Skinner and Feigl, for example) may serve to illustrate the bottom-up strategy, and those of Dennett and Fodor may serve to illustrate the top-down strategy.

Now, Dennett maintains that certain other top-down strategies—in particular, "Freud's ego subsystem," "J. J. Gibson's invariance-sensitive perceptual 'tuning forks,'" "Chomsky's early *syntax*-driven system"—suffer from the danger of stipulating "component subsystems" that have to be "*miraculous.*" They do so, he believes, by "positing more information-processing in a component than the relevant time and matter will allow" or "by positing a subsystem whose duties would require it to be more 'intelligent' or 'knowledgeable' than the supersystem [the molar system] of which it is to be a part."

For the homuncular replacement theory to which he is partial, Dennett's charge would surely stand; but for the model of a complex, functionally differentiated molar system whose own "parts" (as *molar* processing systems) may interact with one another (below the level of consciousness)—the very assumption adopted by Fodor, Chomsky, and others—*no* miracle need be conceded at all (cf. Chomsky, 1979/1980; Freud, 1923/1962; Gibson, 1966).

Since, in Dennett's view, homunculi are first introduced by way of analyzing the molar into *its sub*molar components, it is quite impossible for any homunculus to be endowed with "miraculous" powers; but since, in the opposed view, the molar may *itself* have powers that exceed *its* (own) powers at the level (say) of consciousness, the question of the miraculous simply need not arise. One may, for example, compartmentalize molar discrimination under hypnosis, in such a way that greater acuity of some sort may be manifested in a "part" of the molar agent than is accessible at that agent's conscious level (see Hilgard, 1977). Hence, Dennett appears to have restricted quite arbitrarily the range of theories available to top-down cognitivists. He cannot yet claim to be right (in opposing Fodor) that cognitivist strategies opposed to the homuncular theory are inherently self-defeating and fail to provide scientifically acceptable forms of explanation.

Here is Dennett's (1978a) lucid characterization of homunculi:

One starts, in AI, with a specification of a whole person or cognitive organism—what I call, more neutrally, an intentional system . . . —or some artificial segment of that person's abilities (e.g., chessplaying, answering questions about baseball) and then breaks that largest intentional system into an organization of sub-systems, each of which could itself be viewed as an intentional system (with its own specialized beliefs and desires) and hence as formally a homunculus. . . . If one can get a team or committee of *relatively* ignorant, narrow-minded, blind homunculi to produce the intelligent behavior of the whole, this is progress. . . . Eventually this . . . lands you with homunculi so stupid (all they have to do is remember whether to say yes or no when asked) that they can be, as one says, "replaced by a machine." One *discharges* fancy homunculi from one's scheme by organizing armies of such idiots to do the work.

Some preliminaries are in order. For one thing, homunculi are said to work with "internal representations" of the elements of molar intelligence; but this idiom, Dennett concedes, "is bound to have a large element of metaphor in it." He does not actually say what he takes to be metaphorical or how to replace the metaphorical idiom. What this suggests is that although homuncular analysis is meant to introduce incarnate powers, it is effectively restricted to abstract functional characterizations that may well tempt us to some form of functionalism itself. (There is some evidence that Dennett is attracted in this direction; see Hofstadter & Dennett, 1982). The appeal to metaphor need not complicate matters, however, since, as we shall see, ascriptions to homunculi are conceptually dependent on ascriptions to molar agents—whole persons or cognitive organisms—and ascriptions to the latter are not construed as metaphorical.

Dennett's idiom also draws attention to a critical—perhaps not insurperable—difficulty, namely, that we cannot expect to provide an AI analysis of cognitive abilities without some clear idea of what it means to process internal representations. (We shall return to the issue.) Second, when introduced, homunculi are characterized in intentional terms just as molar persons are. Presumably, speaking in this way is *not* speaking metaphorically, *if* persons are actually intentional systems and if homunculi are real subsystems of real persons. Third, quite independently of the intentional characterization of homunculi, Dennett believes that "fancy" homunculi can be discharged by "stupid" homunculi, and that *all* homunculi can be discharged by eliminating the need to rely on an intentional characterization of the subsystems that produce molar (intentional) activity and behavior. This is the heart of Dennett's reductionism, which begins, first, by conceding the intentional complexity of molar behavior that behaviorists, identity theorists, and other "older" reductive materialists had wrongly supposed they could initially avoid.

We are now in a position to assess Dennett's proposal. In general, there are only three strategies available to cognitivism:

1. the putative subsystems of molar systems may be assigned intentional or informational content purely heuristically;
2. the intentional or informational content of molar states may be analyzed *without remainder* in terms of the informational processing capacities of real homunculi;
3. molar systems are themselves so complex that informational processing *at the molar level* may involve the interaction of relatively independent systems accessible in different ways to one and the same molar agent.

The first strategy is utterly unsatisfactory *if* molar systems are real intentional systems, for either it promises but does not deliver a realistic cognitivism or else it pretends (without adequate argument) that the intentional idiom can actually be replaced or ignored in scientific explanation (cf. Sellars, 1963). The second strategy is the most radical option—Dennett's own *homuncular cognitivism.* It is, as already noted, ultimately meant to yield, at the explanatory level, to some reductive replacement. And the third is the strategy favored by Dennett's "opponents" (Freud, Chomsky, Gibson, Fodor)—that is, *molar cognitivism,* the strategy that favors explanations in which the molar is not replaced by homunculi and in which, therefore, the intentional is not eliminated (at least as far as cognitivism is concerned). Freud (1895/1966), of course, ultimately hoped to eliminate the intentional by a chemical account of libidinal energy and its causal processes; and Fodor (1968) is attracted to some form of the identity theory ("token physicalism," at least; cf. 1975).

The failure of Dennett's strategy seems to be due to an elementary but easily overlooked mistake. Dennett wishes to *replace* all reference to molar or personal-level agency by reference to a suitably complex "committee" of homuncular agents. Nevertheless, based on his own view (and on independent grounds), *the functions of submolar homunculi = the subfunctions of the function of molar agents.* If so, the homuncular *cannot* replace the molar, because the homuncular is nothing but some subroutine *of* the molar itself. There *are* no homunculi *tout court;* there are only homuncular-components-*of*-molar-processes; homunculi are defined relationally in terms of the molar itself. For example, the information processed in the retina or optic nerve pertinent to what a person sees (in the normal sense in which what is seen can be reported) is only *assignable* in relation to whatever component (neural) processes are thought, based on a theory, to bear on the explanation of the informational or intentional content *of the molar perceptual states of that person* (see Gregory, 1966; Polyak, 1941). Thus Dennett (1969) quite reasonably maintains that intentional content "cannot be described" at the homuncular level; it can only be assigned in terms of a teleological model of (say) an organism's life (following Taylor, 1964). So he says quite explicitly (1978b):

> the information or content an event within [a given] system has [it has] *for the system as a* (*biological*) whole. . . . The *content* (in this sense) of a particular vehicle of information, a particular information-bearing event or state, is and must be a function of its function in the system . . . of which it is a part.

Dennett's own account, then, commits him to a version of the third strategy, though he professes to favor the second. Alternatively put, *if* the molar could be physically reduced directly, homuncular reduction would be obviated. But there cannot be any way to reduce the molar by *first* attempting an homuncular reduction, simply because the homuncular is a relational notion that ineliminably involves reference to the molar.

There are two further features of Dennett's account that should be mentioned. First, he claims (1978b) to have constructed "an 'I' . . . out of subpersonal parts of the sort encountered in cognitivistic theories." This is the reason he believes (1969) that:

> . . . the personal story [that is, the "story" of a person's mental states] has a relatively vulnerable and impermanent place in our conceptual scheme, and could in principle be rendered "obsolete" if some day we ceased to *treat* anything (any mobile body or system or device) as an Intentional system—by reasoning with it, communicating with it, etc. (p. 190).

He has somehow forgotten how, in his own view, the intentional characterization of homunculi is and must be assigned; and he has forgotten that *we* must "treat" ourselves reflexively as persons.

Second, Dennett (1971) wrongly supposes (or, at any rate, provides no argument to support his view) that "intentionality is primarily a feature of linguistic entities—idioms, contexts"; that one is not saying "that intentional systems *really* have beliefs and desires, but [only] that one can explain and predict their behavior by ascribing beliefs and desires to them." Here, he seems to be attracted to the first strategy, more or less in accord with Sellars's view. In fact, he (1969) explicitly holds that:

> Intentional objects are not any kind of objects at all. This characteristic is the dependence of Intentional objects on particular descriptions. . . . To change the description is to change the object. What sort of thing is a different thing under different descriptions? Not any object. Can we not do without the objects altogether and talk just of descriptions? (pp. 28–29).

Yes, of course, *but only if the objects can be satisfactorily identified and described in nonintentional terms.* It is in this undefined sense, then, that Dennett (1972/1978) says he wishes "to maintain physicalism . . . but think[s] identity theory is to be shunned."

MOLAR COGNITIVISM AND NATIVISM

Perhaps the most explicit theory instantiating the third strategy appears in Fodor's *The Language of Thought* (1975):

> . . . certain kinds of very central patterns of psychological explanation presuppose the availability *to the behaving organism,* of some sort of representational system. [On

> this view] deciding is a computational process [as in computing the probable consequences of alternative behavioral options and assigning them a preference order]; the act the agent performs is the consequence of computations defined over representations of possible actions. No representations, no computations. No computations, no model. . . . What I am proposing to do is resurrect the traditional notion that there is a "language of thought" and that characterizing that language is a good part of what a theory of the mind needs to do (pp. 31, 33; italics added).

This model clarifies Fodor's reason for confronting Dennett with a dilemma: Either concede a vicious regress of intentional characterizations with respect to homunculi or else drop altogether the homuncular anthropomorphizing of the submolar processes by which molar behavior is to be explained. For his part, Dennett (1977/1978) holds that Fodor's enterprise cannot be saved from "incoherence" except by sharply separating personal-level and subpersonal-level attributions. But, as we have seen: (1) Fodor *does not* admit homuncular agents but only a range of functions of molar agents themselves; and (2) Dennett *cannot* free homuncular ascriptions from a conceptual dependence on molar ascriptions. Here, Fodor surely has the stronger argument: *If* cognitivism is to be sustained, there must be some set of common elements uniting all the functionally distinct processes of molar cognition.

The difficulty with Fodor's theory lies elsewhere. Fodor claims that he is not defending nativism or innatism, merely working out "the consequences of assuming that" psychological processes are computational—in particular, the seemingly unavoidable consequence that if they are computational, then we must have an innately adequate "language" or representational scheme for every cognitive endeavor that we exhibit. We cannot, Fodor (1975) believes, *ever* (in any plausible view of what a concept is) actually learn a new concept: "you cannot learn a language whose terms express semantic properties not expressed by the terms of some language you are already able to use" (p. 61). In effect, learning concepts "is the projection and confirmation of hypotheses"; but if so, then to confirm that a given concept applies presupposes an understanding of the concept in question: We acquire, by learning, only "exemplars" of the concepts we already possess. Fodor's theory, therefore, is a contemporary (genetically grounded) reinterpretation of Plato's doctrine of reminiscence; cognitivism, Fodor is convinced, entails a version of the Platonic theory of concepts.

Nevertheless, there is no evidence (and Fodor offers no evidence) to show: (1) that the entire range of human concepts may be interpreted (even heuristically) as the result of formulable combinations of some finite, relatively economical and manageable set of postulated concepts; or (2) that any promising set of concepts thought to approximate such a reduction could be accounted for in biological terms completely independent of culturally induced learning or acquisition. Actually, Fodor (1975) advances his theory in an even more controversial form. For he maintains:

> If learning a language is literally a matter of making and confirming hypotheses about the truth conditions associated with its predicates, then [it] presupposes the ability to use expressions coextensive with each of the elementary predicates of the language being learned. But . . . the truth conditions associated with *any* predicate of *L* [some natural language *L*] can be expressed in terms of the truth conditions associated with the elementary predicates of *L*. [Hence] one can learn what the semantic properties of a term are only if one already knows a language [one that is not a natural language, a language learned naturally] which contains a term having the same semantic properties" (p. 80; cf. Bruner, 1956).

So construed, the hypothesis-testing model is radically unconfirmed—possibly mistaken, certainly implausible. At the very least, it seems unconvincing to insist that Platonism is inevitable if there is no prospect of formulating the required account in a reasonably detailed way. Very possibly, the acquisition of apparently new concepts cannot be accounted for in terms of computational *learning* (see Fodor, 1979/1980), if Platonism is its unavoidable price.

Fodor views his own thesis as neutral to extensionalist/intensionalist controversies regarding learning or cognizing terms or predicates. For in the extensionalist view (see Davidson, 1967b; Evans & McDowell, 1976), "the semantic properties of a predicate determine its extension" (Fodor, 1975, p. 60) and (Fodor, p. 59, claims) "*S* learns *P* [a predicate in a given language] only if *S* learns a truth rule for *P*" (which apparently requires that one learn a generalization determining the extension of *P*, that is, all the things that *P* is true of.

It is not clear that such a rule *can* be learned or can be shown to have been learned or can be manageably learned with any reasonable measure of reliability or can even be formulated for any natural language. Even if it were true that the meaning of any term could thus be extensionally fixed *in principle,* it would hardly follow that anyone could be said to have learned, or to operate with, such a rule. Certainly, we have no description of *how* concepts are actually thus applied; besides, there are reasonably strong arguments purporting to show that the intension (or meaning or "semantic properties") of a term *do not* determine its extension (see Putnam, 1975). It seems entirely possible that two (semantically) distinct concepts may have the same extension, or at least that they may be known to be distinct, although relative to the constraints of finite testing, they still appear to have the same extension. If so, Fodor cannot be right in holding that learning the meaning of a term is learning the truth-rules governing its extension—independently of the force of the innatist thesis itself. The argument also requires that all learnable languages involve (or be decomposable into) the same set of elementary concepts, that the truth-rules for every learnable language be reducible to some one system of adequate (extensional) truth-rules. But this theory has been strongly opposed (see Hacking, 1975; Quine, 1960), has never been demonstrated, and is not known to be demonstrable. In the intensionalist view (Fodor, 1975), "the semantic properties of a predicate determine its *in*tension and . . . intensions determine extensions" (p. 60)—which is the extensionalist thesis again (see Fodor, 1979/1980).

Fodor acknowledges that some philosophers (notably, Putnam) maintain that the semantic properties of general terms determine neither intensions nor extensions; that on the contrary, what the extension of a term will prove to be depends on the history of empirical discovery—and hence, cannot be innately formed in Fodor's sense. Putnam (1975) also argues: (1) that the meaning of a term "is *not* a function of the psychological state of the speaker by itself"; (2) that "'meanings' just ain't in the head!"; and (3) that the assignment of meanings depends on (an implicit) "*division of linguistic labor*," which itself "rests upon and presupposes the division of nonlinguistic labor." Fodor holds such speculations to be "largely irrelevant." But he fails to see that Putnam is, in effect, sketching an alternative theory of language learning (or language acquisition) and semantic competence. Its effect would be to show that no account of the acquisition or learning of "meanings" *could* be merely computational or cognitivist; for in a spirit not altogether unlike that of such so-called linguistic structuralists as Ferdinand de Saussure (1916/1966) and Louis Hjelmslev (1943/1961) (though for altogether different reasons), Putnam stresses that the semantic dimension of language (doubtless, of other dimensions as well) *cannot be adequately analyzed in any infrapsychological manner at all.* The meaning of what one utters as a speaker of some natural language depends, in large part, on the shifting collective activity and collective experience (nonlinguistic as well as linguistic) of a particular historical society—which it is impossible anyone should have internalized psychologically.

Put paradoxically, the claim is that no one fully understands (or "generates" computationally) the meaning of what one says or does, because the meaning or significance of one's behavior is a function of the implicit consensus or regularities of an *entire* changing society, *interpreting* over time the changing behavior of its members. In Saussure's view, one cannot have internalized the total system of language (*la langue*) in terms of which one's particular utterances (*la parole*) have the linguistic structure they do. Only an entire society can "possess" such a system, and it can possess it only in the heuristic sense that theorists idealize from time to time the structure that actual discourse may be thought to approximate. Actual speech, Saussure believed, did not belong to any finite system at all.

In Wittgenstein's view (1953/1963), no single person can make, follow, or break a rule; rules presuppose the habits of life of an entire society and are, in effect, normative abstractions drawn from the uniformities (and their temporally shifting extensions) that a society shares (or will tolerate). Similarly, among the hermeneutic theorists (see Gadamer, 1960/1975), the understanding of any "text" or utterance cannot be restricted to its supposed "original historical horizon" (the changing but internalized unity of experience of living persons); it inevitably involves a "fusion of horizons," the result of the attempt of those who would understand, to interpret it within their own historically shifting horizon. There is no original to recover. A similar theme appears in Marx's famous Sixth Thesis on Feuerbach: "the human essence is no abstraction inherent in each single individual. In its reality, it is the ensemble of the social relations" (McLellan, 1977; cf. Bourdieu, 1972/1977; Vološinov, 1963; Vygotsky, 1934/1962, 1978).

Here, then, from both analytic and Continental sources, strong reasons may be supplied for distinguishing sharply between the social and infrapsychological dimensions of the mental life of humans. If, for instance, concepts are *second-order* capacities (as Armstrong, 1973, holds), invoked to help organize our explanation of first-order beliefs, then the plausibility of the computational model becomes seriously weakened. It seems quite reasonable to infer internalized *competence* (innate or acquired) from the primary evidence of actual *performance* (see Hamlyn, 1978); but it is odd to suppose that once having constructed our second-order theory thus, we should be able to legislate with confidence about what can have been learned or acquired in the first place. Paul Churchland (1980) very neatly observes that "large-scale learning appears to be identical with conceptual change"—or sufficiently extensive to justify imputations of conceptual change. In any case, since there is no independent access to concepts, there cannot be any empirically justified necessity in restricting concepts innately: Fodor's claim cannot signify more than one theoretical option among others.

The point is also, essentially, Piaget's (see Inhelder & Piaget, 1955/1958). Again, from an entirely different point of view, if it appears difficult or impossible to account for the extended use of general terms (universals) to (new) instances beyond whatever standard cases may first have fixed their sense (for example, *red* or *solid* or *flat* or the like)—without admitting some *consensual* element regarding the acceptability of such an extension (the problem of "pattern recognition": see Rosch, 1973; Smith and Medin, 1981)—then it may be conceptually impossible (or at least extremely unlikely) that the range of human concepts *could* be construed as innately supplied.

For his part, Putnam confirms our profound ignorance of the nature of *learning*. We simply do not know what it is to learn a concept or a new concept. In fact, the Socratic paradox that Fodor resurrects (and that is the heart of his argument) arises only if we explicitly construe learning a concept in a criterial and specifically linguistic way: *S* learns concept *C*; hence, *S* must have known concept *C* in order to learn that concepts $A_1 \ldots A_n$ serve as criterial conditions for *C*. But when the changing behavior of creatures (humans or languageless animals) justifies our holding that they now perform intelligently in a way they could not before, we may speak of their *having learned or acquired a concept that they did not possess before.* The supporting argument must be an inference to the best explanation. If (say) someone develops a grasp of quantum physics, which that person apparently lacked before, *and if* the concepts of quantum physics cannot be "constructed" out of a supposed innate supply of concepts, then we may reasonably claim that in learning quantum physics, the person "learned" or "acquired" a concept that he or she did not have before. The mere coherence of the alternative shows that in contrast to what he says, Fodor is not actually driven to Platonism. On the face of it, it seems quite preposterous to suppose that *all* culturally rich concepts are nothing more than combinations (of some unexplained sort) of some genetically, preculturally determined range of original concepts.

It needs to be said that a cognitive model could, coherently, admit some (conceivably quite restricted) innate capacities, some culturally or socially acquired conceptual abilities (duly internalized), and some concession to the interpretive, consensual social work that Putnam, Wittgenstein, Saussure, Marx, Gadamer, and others have (in their different ways) affirmed. This concession, of course, is incompatible with an exclusive cognitivism—and generates fresh difficulties of its own. But there is no reason to restrict cognitivism to mere innate capacities, and there are no good grounds for supposing that it could be adequate to its problem.

DIFFICULTIES WITH NATIVISM

Pertinent objections may be pressed here against Chomsky, who has argued, along lines rather different from Fodor's, the empirical necessity of conceding innate linguistic competence. By *competence,* Chomsky means an innately organized, species-specific capacity to apply to some cognitively significant sector of behavior or discrimination (the functional parts of language or perception, say) a system of universal rules (a grammar or analogous regularities) that are not introspectively accessible (see Chomsky, 1980). Clearly, competence is independent of, underlies, but need never be manifested in any form of *performance;* the underlying rules of linguistic performance, for instance, may well constitute a different "pragmatic" competence. It is essential to Chomsky's view that the forms of (innate) competence are specialized in a modular, somewhat tasklike way and are *not* manifestations of a general (innate) intelligence.

Here, in effect, Chomsky provides an extremely useful way of distinguishing between classical empiricism and rationalism. For contrary to the impression conveyed by Locke's *tabula rasa,* empiricism *is* committed to some form of innate cognitive structure (some form of general intelligence). Quine (1969) makes the same point quite tellingly:

> . . . whatever we may make of Locke, the behaviorist is knowingly and cheerfully up to his neck in innate mechanisms of learning-readiness. The very reinforcement and extinction of responses, so central to behaviorism, depends on prior inequalities in the subject's qualitative spacing, so to speak, of stimulations. . . .

The proper question regarding nativism, then, concerns only *the extent and nature of the innate mechanisms* that govern language acquisition (or perception or action or the like); the rule to be favored must be some version of parsimony since all relevant arguments are inferences to the best explanation (see Chomsky, 1967; Goodman, 1967; Putnam, 1967).

Chomsky (1980) stresses that in his own view, "the mind is a highly differentiated [modular] structure, with quite distinct subsystems. If so, an understanding of the properties of one of these systems should not be expected to provide the principles by which others are organized and function" (p. 27). The point is that *if*, say, the underlying structure of language is biologically determined, then on the evidence of what would be required to account for its complexity, language (as well as other mental powers) would have to be a network of specialized competences. This explains part of Chomsky's resistance to AI modeling, which is more empiricist than rationalist and favors general intelligence over specialized (modular) competences (Chomsky, 1979/1980; cf. Leiber, 1975).

Difficulties abound, however. First, Chomsky has never provided a full account of the way in which a system of innate competences and successful performance actually mesh. Given the nature of the argument, it is somewhat premature to deny the role of innate general intelligence or its bearing on various sorts of successful performance. Second, there are those who argue, particularly with regard to language (conceivably, in a way that could be generalized), that no grammar can be assigned as *the* grammar of a natural language (see Chomsky, 1977/1979; Harris, 1951/1961). But Chomsky is willing to countenance a certain idealization here, consistent with the biological realism he advocates and consistent with his conviction that there *is* empirical evidence differentially favoring "specific theories of language universals" (Chomsky, 1980; cf. Stich, 1978). Third, it may be possible to argue, particularly with respect to language, that there may be *sub*linguistic competences important enough to account, together with innate general intelligence, for the convergent patterns of natural language.

This last statement may seem a quibble, but what it shows is that concessions to *general* intelligence go hand in hand with the thesis that language is in large part *culturally acquired.* Since Chomsky himself stresses that the empirical evidence favoring innate competences lies with considerations like that of "the poverty of the stimulus"—the remarkable speed, for instance, with which children learn their languages from fragmented and even defective specimens, or the convergence of the underlying grammatical structure of all natural languages (partly idealized, possibly even an artifact of theorizing about linguistic uniformities; Chomsky, 1979/1980)—and that the evidence does not lie with fitting such competence closely to the actual performances of native speakers, it proves to be quite difficult to construe the argument between Chomsky and his opponents as empirically straightforward.

This difficulty does not seem to affect in the least, however, the empirical confirmation of particular regularities that Chomsky and his co-workers have affirmed. But on the question of sublinguistic competences, there is some quite curious evidence that distinctly nonlanguage-using animals, chinchillas, for instance, can be trained to differentiate specialized phonetic features of speech, to generalize over novel instances, and to demarcate speech stimuli (that do not rest on clearly demarcated acoustical segments) within the same range as humans (see Juhl & Miller, 1975; also, Liberman, 1967). This is no argument, of course, but it does show the plausibility of pursuing explanations substantially opposed to Chomsky's. Fourth, some will see in the very admission of linguistic *rules* an implicit concession, on Chomsky's part, of a form of general intelligence—rather along the lines, already noted, of Wittgenstein's way of connecting social practices and idealized rules.

A deeper objection arises, however, possibly the most fundamental, as far as the empirical study of language and analogous systems is concerned. It questions the biological priority and autonomy of a universal grammar, and it lends substance to the smaller objections just tabulated. Chomsky himself (1977/1979; cf. Chomsky, 1957; Jackendoff, 1972) formulates the difficulty in the most candid and compelling way:

> . . . linguistic theory (or "universal grammar") is . . . a genetically determined property of the species: the child does not learn this theory, but rather applies it in developing knowledge of language. . . . [But if] nonlinguistic factors [must be included in] grammar: beliefs, attitudes, etc., [this would] amount to a rejection of the initial idealization to language, as an object of study. A priori, such a move cannot be ruled out, but it must be empirically motivated. If it proves to be correct, I would conclude that language is a chaos that is not worth studying. . . . Note that the question is not whether belief or attitudes, and so on, play a role in linguistic behavior or linguistic judgments . . . [but rather] whether distinct cognitive structures can be identified, which interact in the real use of language and linguistic judgments, the grammatical system being one of these (pp. 140, 152–153).

In effect, if reference, speech act contexts, nonlinguistic factors of experience and behavior, social practices, and semantic and pragmatic aspects of linguistic use essentially affect the development of the grammar of a natural language—if the "surface" and "deep" features of a language cannot be systematically sorted to insure the independence of innate generative rules, or if the syntactic dimension of language cannot be insured a measure of autonomy relative to aspects of language clearly dependent on contingent learning, or if the systems of competence and performance cannot be independently sorted—then, in Chomsky's view, "language is a chaos." Of course, it would not be a chaos, in the obvious sense that it would remain subject to empirical analysis. But it would entail that the mind could not be a network of modular, genetically programmed competences of the sort Chomsky envisages; it would entail the work of innate general intelligence—and hence, of the social contingencies of language acquisition. And that would signify, based on an argument provided shortly before, that language could not convincingly be accounted for on nativist or, more generally, on cognitivist grounds.

BEYOND COGNITIVISM

We are at the end of the argument, now, having traced a succession of the principal conceptual strategies of cognitive psychology within the Anglo-American tradition. They have all been found seriously defective. If, then, in closing, we should at least consider some of the more promising directions psychological theory may be expected to pursue, however inchoate these may appear at the present time, it would be best to be brief. Two themes suggest themselves. One is the direct consequence of the inadequacy of cognitivism, namely, that there are no plausible or compelling grounds for postulating a psychologically internalized system capable of generating *all* the cognitively pertinent behavior of human agents. The other identifies the single most salient feature of human intelligence and its scientific study, either neglected or positively opposed by the four movements we have been tracing, namely, what we may now call the *consensual* nature of psychology and the so-called human sciences (sociology, linguistics, art history, and the like). The two are actually closely related and permit us to specify, quite economically, any number of conceptual puzzles that a more adequate psychology may be expected to resolve. One may well ask why these issues have not been systematically explored within the philosophy of psychology, if they are so readily mentioned. The simple answer seems to be that psychology has long been in the thrall of explanatory models that systematically excluded them and that have sought to confirm the adequacy of the methods of inquiry originally suited to the physical sciences.

A few illustrations of this tendency related to the issues we have already explored will orient us effectively. For example, in advancing his rather unusual version of nativism, Chomsky (1980) rejects in a telltale way what has been dubbed "the bifurcation thesis" (see Hockney, 1975), roughly, the thesis that there is a systematic methodological difference between the natural sciences and the so-called human sciences (intended to include linguistics and psychology). In opposing Piaget's view of cognitive development, Chomsky says (1979/1980):

> It is a curiosity of our intellectual history that cognitive structures developed by the mind are generally regarded and studied very differently from physical structures developed by the body. There is no reason why a neutral scientist, unencumbered by traditional doctrine, should adopt this view. Rather, he would, or should approach cognitive structures such as human language more or less as he would investigate an organ such as the eye or heart. . . (p. 37).

Certainly, it is most unusual to treat language as an organ system. We have absolutely no clear notion of how to study the "development" or "evolution" of that organ in detailed genetic and physiological terms. Chomsky (1980) intends in part to offer a basis for holding that "in certain fundamental respects we do not really learn language; rather, grammar grows in the mind" (p. 134). This, too, threatens to be a misleading metaphor. But what is more important is Chomsky's insistence that the human studies may not be significantly different, methodologically, from the physical and biological sciences. However, if the force of the foregoing arguments is conceded, Chomsky must be essentially mistaken: There *is* a point to the bifurcation thesis, though to admit it is not to deny the continuity of the physical and human sciences in the analysis of what we have called incarnate phenomena.

The point is that at the level at which human psychology, human language, and human culture are examined, the pertinent disciplines must be *consensual* in the conjoint sense: (1) that the distinctive phenomena in question exist only insofar as a human community actually shares linguistic and cultural practices; (2) that those practices cannot be described or accounted for solely in terms of the infrapsychological powers of the aggregated members of such a community; and (3) that paradigmatically (at least), the scientific observers of such phenomena are (and must be) themselves apt participants in those same practices. In the physical sciences, although investigation itself cannot fail to involve consensus, the (merely) physical world that we investigate is presumed to be a structured, causally effective world—lacking intentional properties altogether—*that exists independently of our inquiries*. There is, however, nothing to explore in that emergent increment of the world that language and human culture first make possible except what, as apt agents within a particular historical society, we *both* generate and observe—*and* understand in essentially the same way in those two roles.

The physical sciences must, of course, function consensually in formulating a reasonably objective view of the physical world; but the domain to be explained is conceded to exist independently of human inquiry itself. Consequently, the physical sciences strive to reduce as far as possible the distorting role of our contingent cognitive interests. But the human sciences cannot favor a comparable presupposition. Whatever objectivity may be claimed for them depends precisely on reducing the distortion *of* a consensual and reflexive understanding of one's own culturally formed practices, that is, of a domain that exists only *as* a system of consensual practices and the artifacts it generates. Objectivity, therefore, with respect to language and the culturally shaped mental life of human beings essentially depends on our acquiring a *natural* aptitude both to observe and to generate the relevant sorts of behavior. Here "natural" simply means what accords with that form of consensus—more or less in the Wittgensteinian sense already sketched—in which we first learn from infancy to behave conformably with practices already in place in a particular historical community, so that, gradually, we contribute spontaneously to the continuing evolution of those same practices.

To attempt to describe in detail the full complexities of this phenomenon would require an entirely fresh beginning. But if, for example, Chomsky were (and could be shown to be) mistaken in supposing that the grammar of a language can be prised apart from its semantic features—so that a genetic and biologically developmental account can be suitably given of that module of a language—and if he were mistaken in supposing that the grammatical and semantic features of a language can be prised apart from the entire range of nonlinguistic experience acquired contingently, diachronically, and variably, then the full import of insisting on the consensual nature of the human sciences would be easily confirmed. Certainly, the notion that language is essentially or primarily like an internal organ of the body would be exposed as the profoundly misleading image that it is.

Viewed against the backdrop of the arguments and conceptual distinctions already mustered, the consequences would be considerable. For example, our theory of causality and of causal explanation would be seriously affected. We would have to concede (notably, against Davidson, 1970), that in the cultural context, causes could not be reduced physicalistically and could not always (or even characteristically) be identified in an extensionally reliable way, as by correlating incarnate causes with the regularities of the physical events in which they were incarnated. Thus, an action of insulting another is a culturally distinctive activity normally acknowledged to have causal significance. Yet there is no obvious way in which to identify acts of insulting, in physically regularized respects; there seems to be no way in which such acts can be specified at all, except intensionally. But it is a familiar canon of causal theory that causal contexts invariably behave extensionally. If, furthermore, singular causes can be recognized as such (as most discussants admit), without reference to the causal laws they are supposed to instantiate, and if they can be specified only intensionally, it becomes problematic (again, *contra* Davidson) whether all causal relations are and must be lawlike: The regularities of a certain society's practice of insulting may well be perceptible; but it hardly follows that such regularities would ever yield causal laws, simply because they would themselves be seen as causally shaped and altered (in ways specifiable only intensionally) within the developing history of that same society. In short, the uniformities of culturally specific causes might be (intensionally) formulated only as "covering institutions" rather than (extensionally) as covering laws (see Margolis, 1983; cf. Beauchamp & Rosenberg, 1981).

Institutions—practices, traditions, and the like—seem to have the peculiar property, first of all, that unlike causal laws, they are themselves the result of causal forces; second, that they afford sufficient regularity, within given social and historical contexts, so that particular behavior and work can be causally explained by reference to them; and third, that if our earlier arguments about the irreducibility of the intentional and intensional features of human life are sustained, there is no methodologically viable alternative to such explanation. This would lead to quite heterodox views of the scientific status of psychology and the other human disciplines, or else to the denial that they were sciences at all. But, in contrast to Chomsky, the bifurcation thesis would be vindicated.

Consider another illustration. The Danish theorist of language, Louis Hjelmslev (1943/1961) maintains that "*A priori* it would seem to be a generally valid thesis that for every *process* there is a corresponding *system*, by which the process can be analyzed and described by means of a limited number of premises" (p. 9). In a way not unlike that in which (as we have seen) Putnam regards everything as a probabilistic automaton under some description, Hjelmslev believes that "a general and exhaustive calculus of the possible combinations" of some limited number of elements could be constructed for every system, so that all the events internal to that system could be "foreseen and the conditions for their realization established." The result, he thinks, would be "a systematic, exact, and generalizing science."

Hjelmslev's thesis is a classic version of what is now termed *structuralism*, of which cognitivism may now be regarded as that version restricted to infrapsychological systems. Two important qualifications of Hjelmslev's thesis deserve to be noted. First, systems formulated in the manner he details need not be infrapsychological or exclusively infrapsychological; they may, for instance, be *social*. Very much in Saussure's sense (already noted), Hjelmslev treats language as a system successfully used by an entire society rather than merely as infrapsychologically generated. Second, in Hjelmslev's view, such a system would probably be "arbitrary" (since there may be many alternative theories of what such a system could be like relative to a set of generated practices, and since such theories need not be construed as postulating real psychological or social processes); it would also be "appropriate" (since such theories would facilitate empirically testable claims).

In effect, what Hjelmslev's thesis shows is, first, that even if there were a representational mechanism of some sort that could generate all cognitively significant behavior (in the way Fodor and Dennett rather differently suppose), the mechanism might be "internalized" only socially; and second, that to construe behavior as cognitively significant only relative to such a representational mechanism (a grammar or a set of social institutions or the like) would *not* commit one to the actual existence of such a mechanism. It would be entirely possible that only *part* of such a mechanism would have to be realized infrapsychologically, that systemlike, partial schemata of Hjelmslev's sort may be (and may need to be) imposed both prospectively *and* retrospectively *in interpreting the cognitive import of particular agents' behavior.* This concept would fit very well, for instance, with the consensual nature of social existence that (as we saw) Wittgenstein emphasizes. The schemata in question might, then, be relatively incomplete, divergent or convergent within tolerable limits relative to a finite run of actual behavior, diachronically replaced in accordance with shifting perceptions of shifting patterns of behavior, and compatible with improvisations consensually tolerated by the members of a particular society. In short, Hjelmslev's structuralism shows (against its own intent) the coherence of accounting for cognitively significant "processes" *without* an underlying total "system."

Two further consequences follow. For one, it cannot be necessary that the generative "system" ascribed to apt agents at the moment of their behaving one way or another be the same as the "system" ascribed any agent (the same or another) who may be said to understand or interpret the import of that same behavior. Second, although the mental must be incarnated, ascriptions of intentional import to particular actions need not be distributively assigned incarnating neurophysiological states; they may be justified solely by reference to the holistic requirements of some generative model of rationality. For example, young children, in the process of first learning their native tongue, utter what is not explicitly a complete sentence but which, in context, may be fairly understood in a variety of plausible ways ("'nana," say, pointing with some excitement to a banana). Consider, then, that discourse and behavior of a distinctly improvisational sort *at any stage in the mastery of social practices* will exhibit these same features. So seen, cognitive phenomena are probably rarely *cognitivistic* (in the full sense examined), but are more nearly *cognignomic* (in the sense that they justifiably invite interpretation in accordance with the practices of a society) and *cognigenic* (in the sense that they issue from the exercise of cognitive powers and invite cognitively pertinent responses). The human sciences, then, will exhibit a strongly interpretive tendency, tolerant, within somewhat generous limits, of alternative, diachronically shifting, approximately complete, idealized generative systems. Here, again, the contrast featured in the "bifurcation thesis" proves well-nigh impossible to deny.

Notice that it is the demonstrated weaknesses of the principal theories of cognitive psychology that have driven us to concede that the human sciences—psychology and the social and cultural disciplines—may well be significantly different from the physical sciences, both methodologically and ontologically. Language appears to be *sui generis;* essential to the actual aptitudes of human beings; irreducible to physical processes; inexplicable solely infrapsychologically; real only as embedded in the practices of an historical society; identifiable consensually or only in terms that presuppose consensual practices linking observer and observed; inseparable as far as meaning is concerned from the changing, novel, nonlinguistic experience of a people; incapable of being formulated as a closed system of rules; subject always to the need for improvisational interpretation and, therefore, subject also to ineliminable psychological indeterminacies regarding intention and action. These features of language infect all distinctly human aptitudes, since the latter are "lingual" even where they are not narrowly linguistic—that is, insofar as, like waging war, dancing, and building bridges, they are aptitudes that presuppose linguistic ability (Ricoeur, 1981).

What is most remarkable about them is that, once mentioned, they impress us as either strongly plausible or reasonably settled or, at the very least, as important possibilities that we cannot justifiably ignore. Nevertheless, as a review of the foregoing arguments confirms, they are features that have been all but neglected by the dominant movements of the philosophy of psychology in the Anglo-American tradition. We must realize, therefore, that the upshot of our analysis, if it were strongly supported by independent investigators, would be to invite a quite radical departure in the conceptual orientation of empirical psychology itself.

There is in fact one very large thesis, increasingly salient in the social and cultural disciplines but hardly acknowledged at all in the psychological literature, that collects in a powerfully unified way all the features of linguistic and lingual phenomena that have just been mentioned. That is the thesis that the emerging forms of human consciousness are ineliminably *praxical,* that is, causally grounded in and reflecting the historically changing and evolving activities of socially organized labor. The doctrine is classically linked with Marx's *Theses on Feuerbach;* but, as in the influential theories of Heidegger (1962/1977) and Dewey (1917), it is reasonably clear both that social *praxis* need not take an exclusively Marxist form and that it is itself a decidedly problematic concept. The point of pressing the praxical theme here is simply to show how readily the conceptual thrust of the entire tradition we have examined could be quite radically—and promisingly—altered; and how, in adjusting the tradition thus, we should then have to consider, within the scope of psychological theory, the full implications of treating human nature as open to fundamental processes of historical change. That idea—that inquiry into human psychology is itself subject to the organizing conceptual constraints of praxically different historically contexts not always, be it noted, open to ready identification by those who are then inquiring—is surely both the most radical and the least examined possibility affecting the status of psychology as a science.

We cannot, here, pursue these dawning possibilities. They are offered more in the spirit of prospects largely overlooked than of findings confirmed. Nevertheless, the mere coherence and promise of these neglected options show, once the difficulties of the four principal movements of cognitive theory be conceded, that psychology may well be inseparable from the social and historical sciences and much more akin to such interpretive disciplines as, say, literary criticism than could be admitted by those attracted to the canons of the unity of science program. In any event, these possibilities emerge in a noticeably natural way from a close examination of the claims of the principal theories of our own day.

References

ALBRITTON, R. On Wittgenstein's use of the term "criterion." *Journal of Philosophy,* 1959, *56.*

APEL, K.-O. *The transformation of philosophy.* G. Adey & D. Frisby, trans. London: Routledge & Kegan Paul, 1972/1980.

ARMSTRONG, D. M. *Bodily sensations.* London: Routledge & Kegan Paul, 1962.

ARMSTRONG, D. M. *A materialist theory of the mind.* London: Routledge & Kegan Paul, 1968.

ARMSTRONG, D. M. *Belief, truth and knowledge.* Cambridge, England: Cambridge University Press, 1973.

BEAUCHAMP, T. L., & ROSENBERG, A. *Hume and the problem of causation.* New York: Oxford University Press, 1981.

BLOCK, N. Troubles with functionalism. In C. W. Savage (Ed.), *Minnesota Studies in the Philosophy of Science* (Vol. 9). Minneapolis: University of Minnesota Press, 1978.

BLOCK, N. Psychologism and behaviorism. *Philosophical Review,* 1981, *90.*

BLOCK, N., & FODOR, J. A. What psychological states are not. *Philosophical Review,* 1972, *81.*

BODEN, M. A. *Purposive explanation in psychology.* Cambridge, Mass.: Harvard University Press, 1972.

BODEN, M. A. *Artificial intelligence and natural man.* New York: Basic Books, 1977.

BOGEN, J. E. The other side of the brain I: Dysgraphia and dyscopia following cerebral commissurotomy. *Bulletins of the Los Angeles Neurological Society,* 1969, *34.* (a)

Bogen, J. E. The other side of the brain II: An appositional mind. *Bulletins of the Los Angeles Neurological Society,* 1969, *34.* (b)

Bourdieu, P. *Outline of a theory of practice.* R. Nice, trans. Cambridge, England: Cambridge University Press, 1972/1977.

Brandt, R., & Kim, J. The logic of the identity theory. *Journal of Philosophy,* 1967, *64.*

Brentano, F. The distinction between mental and physical phenomena. In O. Kraus (Ed.), *Psychology from an empirical standpoint* (English edition, Ed. L. L. McAlister). London: Routledge & Kegan Paul, 1874/1973.

Broad, C. D. *The mind and its place in nature.* London: Routledge & Kegan Paul, 1925.

Brodbeck, M. Mental and physical: Identity versus sameness. In P. K. Feyerabend & G. Maxwell (Eds.), *Mind, matter, and method.* Minneapolis: University of Minnesota Press, 1966.

Bruner, J. S., Goodnow, J. J., & Austin, G. A. *A study of thinking.* New York: Wiley, 1956.

Carnap, R. *The unity of science.* M. Black, trans. London: Kegan Paul, 1931/1934.

Carnap, R. *The logical syntax of language.* New York: Harcourt, Brace, 1937.

Carnap, R. Psychology in physical language. G. Schick, trans. In A. J. Ayer (Ed.), *Logical positivism.* Glencoe, Ill.: Free Press, 1932–1933/1959.

Causey, R. L. *Unity of science.* Dordrecht, Holland: Reidel, 1977.

Chisholm, R. M. *Perceiving.* Ithaca, N.Y.: Cornell University Press, 1957.

Chisholm, R. M. *Theory of knowledge.* Englewood Cliffs, N.J.: Prentice-Hall, 1966/1976.

Chomsky, N. *Syntactic structures.* The Hague: Mouton, 1957.

Chomsky, N. Review of B. F. Skinner, *Verbal behavior. Language,* 1959, *35.*

Chomsky, N. *Cartesian linguistics.* New York: Harper & Row, 1966.

Chomsky, N. Recent contributions to the theory of innate ideas. *Synthese,* 1967, *17.*

Chomsky, N. *Language and responsibility.* J. Viertel, trans. New York: Pantheon, 1977/1979.

Chomsky, N. On cognitive structures and their development: A reply to Piaget. In M. Piattelli-Palmarini (Ed.), *Language and learning: The debate between Jean Piaget and Noam Chomsky.* Cambridge, Mass.: Harvard University Press, 1979/1980.

Chomsky, N. *Rules and representations.* New York: Columbia University Press, 1980.

Churchland, P. M. Plasticity: Conceptual and neuronal. *Behavioral and Brain Sciences,* 1980, *3.*

Cornman, J. The identity of mind and body. *Journal of Philosophy,* 1962, *59.* (a)

Cornman, J. Intentionality and intensionality. *Philosophical Quarterly,* 1962, *12.* (b)

Cornman, J. Mental terms, theoretical terms, and materialism. *Philosophy of Science,* 1968, *34.* (a)

Cornman, J. On the elimination of "sensations" and sensations. *Review of Metaphysics,* 1968, *20.* (b)

Davidson, D. Causal relations. *Journal of Philosophy,* 1967, *64.* (a)

DAVIDSON, D. Truth and meaning. *Synthese,* 1967, *17.* (b)

DAVIDSON, D. Mental events. In L. Foster & J. W. Swanson (Eds.), *Experience & theory.* Amherst: University of Massachusetts Press, 1970.

DAVIDSON, D. Agency. In R. Binkley et al. (Eds.), *Agent, action, and reason.* Toronto: University of Toronto Press, 1971.

DAVIDSON, D. Thought and talk. In S. Guttenplan (Ed.), *Mind and language.* New York: Oxford University Press, 1975.

DAWKINS, R. *The selfish gene.* New York: Oxford University Press, 1976.

DENNETT, D. C. *Content and consciousness.* London: Routledge & Kegan Paul, 1969.

DENNETT, D. C. Intentional systems. *Journal of Philosophy,* 1971, *68.*

DENNETT, D. C. Reply to Arbib and Gunderson. *Brainstorms.* Montgomery, Vt.: Bradford Books, 1972/1978.

DENNETT, D. C. A cure for the common code? *Brainstorms.* Montgomery, Vt.: Bradford Books, 1977/1978.

DENNETT, D. C. Artificial intelligence as philosophy and as psychology. In M. Ringle (Ed.), *Philosophical perspectives in artificial intelligence.* Atlantic Highlands, N.J.: Humanities Press, 1978. (a)

DENNETT, D. C. Toward a cognitive theory of consciousness. In C. W. Savage (Ed.), *Minnesota Studies in the Philosophy of Science* (Vol. 9). Minneapolis: University of Minnesota Press, 1978. (b)

DEWEY, J. The need for a recovery of philosophy. In J. Dewey et al., *Creative intelligence: Essays in the pragmatic attitude.* New York: Henry Holt, 1917.

DREYFUS, H. L. *What computers can't do* (Rev. ed.). New York: Harper & Row, 1972/1979.

ECCLES, J. C. *Facing reality.* New York: Springer-Verlag, 1970.

ESTES, W. K. Stimulus–response theory of drive. In M. R. Jones (Ed.), *Nebraska Symposium on Motivation.* Lincoln: University of Nebraska Press, 1958.

EVANS, G., & MCDOWELL, J. (EDS.). *Truth and meaning.* Oxford, England: Clarendon, 1976.

FAHLMAN, S. E. *NETL: A system for representing and using real-world knowledge.* Cambridge, Mass.: MIT Press, 1979.

FEIGENBAUM, E. A., & FELDMAN, J. (EDS.). *Computers and thought.* New York: McGraw-Hill, 1963.

FEIGL, H. *The "mental" and the "physical": The essay and a postscript.* Minneapolis: University of Minnesota Press, 1958/1967.

FEYERABEND, P. Materialism and the mind-body problem. *Review of Metaphysics,* 1963, *17.* (a)

FEYERABEND, P. Mental events and the brain. *Journal of Philosophy,* 1963, *60.* (b)

FEYERABEND, P. *Against method.* London: NLB, 1975.

FODOR, J. A. *Psychological explanation.* New York: Random House, 1968.

FODOR, J. A. *The language of thought.* New York: Crowell, 1975.

FODOR, J. A. On the impossibility of acquiring "more powerful" structures. In M. Piattelli-Palmarini (Ed.), *Language and learning: The debate between Jean Piaget and Noam Chomsky.* Cambridge, Mass.: Harvard University Press, 1979/1980.

FØLLESDAL, D. Husserl's notion of noema. *Journal of Philosophy,* 1969, *66.*

FREUD, S. Project for a scientific psychology. In *The standard edition of the complete psychological works of Sigmund Freud* (Vol. 1, 1886–1899). J. Strachey et al., trans. London: Hogarth Press and the Institute of Psycho-analysis, 1895/1966.

FREUD, S. *The ego and the id.* J. Riviere, trans.; rev. J. Strachey. New York: Norton, 1923/1962.

GADAMER, H.-G. *Truth and method.* G. Barden & J. Cumming, trans. from 2nd ed. New York: Seabury Press, 1960/1975.

GAZZANIGA, M. S. (ED.). *Handbook of behavioral neurobiology* (Vol. 2). New York: Plenum, 1979.

GEACH, P. T. *Mental acts.* London: Routledge & Kegan Paul, 1957.

GIBSON, E. J., & WALK, R. D. The visual cliff. *Scientific American,* 1960, *202.*

GIBSON, J. J. *The senses considered as perceptual systems.* Boston: Houghton Mifflin, 1966.

GIBSON, J. J. *The ecological approach to visual perception.* Boston: Houghton Mifflin, 1979.

GOODMAN, N. *The structure of appearance* (2nd ed.). Indianapolis, Ind.: Bobbs-Merrill, 1951/1966.

GOODMAN, N. *Fact, fiction, and forecast* (2nd ed.). Indianapolis, Ind.: Bobbs-Merrill, 1955/1965.

GOODMAN, N. The epistemological argument. *Synthese,* 1967, *17.*

GREGORY, R. L. *Eye and brain.* New York: McGraw-Hill, 1966.

HACKING, I. *Why does language matter to philosophy?* Cambridge, England: Cambridge University Press, 1975.

HALDANE, E. S., & ROSS, G.T.R. (TRANS.). *The philosophical works of Descartes* (corr. ed.). Cambridge, England: Cambridge University Press, 1911–1912/1934.

HAMLYN, D. W. *Experience and the growth of understanding.* London: Routledge & Kegan Paul, 1978.

HARMAN, G. *Thought.* Princeton, N.J.: Princeton University Press, 1973.

HARRIS, Z. S. *Structural linguistics.* Chicago: University of Chicago Press, 1951/1961.

HAUGELAND, J. The nature and plausibility of cognitivism. *Behavioral and Brain Sciences,* 1978, *1.*

HAUGELAND, J. The nature and plausibility of cognitivism—Author's response. *Behavioral and Brain Sciences,* 1979, *2.*

HEIDEGGER, M. The question concerning technology. In *The question concerning technology and other essays,* W. Lovitt, trans. New York: Harper & Row, 1962/1977.

HILGARD, E. R. Toward a neo-dissociative theory: Multiple cognitive controls in human functioning. *Perspectives in Biology and Medicine,* 1974, *17.*

HILGARD, E. R. *Divided consciousness.* New York: Wiley, 1977.

HILGARD, E. R., & BOWER, G. H. *Theories of learning* (4th ed.). Englewood Cliffs, N.J.: Prentice-Hall, 1975.

HJELMSLEV, L. *Prolegomena to a theory of language* (Rev. ed.). F. J. Whitfield, trans. Madison: University of Wisconsin Press, 1943/1961.

HOCKNEY, D. The bifurcation of scientific theories and indeterminacy of translation. *Philosophy of Science,* 1975, *42.*

HOFSTADTER, D. R., & DENNETT, D. C. (EDS.). *The mind's I: Fantasies and reflections on self and soul.* New York: Basic Books, 1982.

HOLT, E. B. *Animal drive and the learning process.* New York: Holt, Rinehart & Winston, 1931.

HULL, C. L. *Principles of behavior.* New York: Appleton-Century-Crofts, 1943.

HUSSERL, E. *Ideas: General introduction to pure phenomenology.* W.R.B. Gibson, trans. New York: Macmillan, 1931.

INHELDER, B., & PIAGET, J. *The growth of logical thinking from childhood to adolescence.* A. Parsons & S. Milgram, trans. New York: Basic Books, 1955/1958.

JACKENDOFF, R. S. *Semantic interpretation in generative grammar.* Cambridge, Mass.: MIT Press, 1972.

JUHL, P. K., & MILLER, J. D. Speech perception by the chinchilla: Voiced–voiceless distinction in aveolar plosive consonants. *Science,* 1975, *190.*

KAUFMAN, A. S. Behaviorism. In P. Edwards (Ed.), *The encyclopedia of philosophy* (Vol. 1). New York: Macmillan, 1967.

KENNY, A. *Action, emotion and will.* London: Routledge & Kegan Paul, 1963.

KÖRNER, S. *Experience and theory.* London: Routledge & Kegan Paul, 1966.

KUHN, T. S. *The structure of scientific revolutions* (2nd ed. enl.). Chicago: University of Chicago Press, 1962/1970.

KUHN, T. S. *The essential tension.* Chicago: University of Chicago Press, 1977.

LACEY, H. The scientific study of linguistic behavior: A perspective on the Skinner–Chomsky controversy. *Journal for the Theory of Social Behavior,* 1974, *4.*

LACEY, H. Skinner on the prediction and control of behavior. *Theory and Decision,* 1978, *10.*

LAKATOS, I. The methodology of scientific research programmes. In J. Worrall & G. Currie (Eds.), *Philosophical papers* (Vol. 1). Cambridge, England: Cambridge University Press, 1978.

LEIBER, J. *Noam Chomsky: A philosophical overview.* New York: St. Martin's Press, 1975.

LEVIN, M. E. *Metaphysics and the mind–body problem.* Oxford, England: Clarendon, 1979.

LEWIS, D. K. An argument for the identity theory. *Journal of Philosophy,* 1966, *63.*

LIBERMAN, A. M. ET AL. Perception of the speech code. *Psychological Review,* 1967, *74.*

LORENZ, K. *Studies in animal and human behavior* (2 vols.). R. Martin, trans. Cambridge, Mass.: Harvard University Press, 1970.

MALCOLM, N. Wittgenstein's *Philosophical investigations. Philosophical Review,* 1954, *63.*

MALCOLM, N. Behaviorism as a philosophy of psychology. In T. W. Wann (Ed.), *Behaviorism and phenomenology: Contrasting bases for modern psychology.* Chicago: University of Chicago Press, 1964.

MALCOLM, N. Thoughtless brutes. *Proceedings and Addresses of the American Philosophical Association* (1972–73), 1973, *46*.

MARGOLIS, J. Arguments with intensional and extensional features. *Southern Journal of Philosophy,* 1977, *15*. (a)

MARGOLIS, J. The stubborn opacity of belief contexts. *Theoria,* 1977, *43*. (b)

MARGOLIS, J. *Persons and minds.* Dordrecht, Holland: Reidel, 1978. (a)

MARGOLIS, J. Reconciling Freud's *Scientific project* and psychoanalysis. In H. T. Engelhardt, Jr. & D. Callahan (Eds.), *Morals, science and sociality* (*The foundations of ethics and its relationship to science*) (Vol. III). Hastings-on-Hudson, N.Y.: The Hastings Center, 1978. (b)

MARGOLIS, J. *Art and philosophy.* Atlantic Highlands, N.J.: Humanities Press, 1980.

MARGOLIS, J. *Culture and cultural entities: Toward a new unity of science.* Dordrecht, Holland: Reidel, 1983.

MCCARTHY, J. Ascribing mental qualities to machines. In M. Ringle (Ed.), *Philosophical perspectives in artificial intelligence.* Atlantic Highlands, N.J.: Humanities Press, 1979.

MCDOUGALL, W. Modern materialism. *Bedrock,* 1913, *2*.

MCLELLAN, D. *Karl Marx: Selected writings.* London: Oxford University Press, 1977.

MEEHL, P. E., & SELLARS, W. The concept of emergence. In H. Feigl & M. Scriven (Eds.), *Minnesota Studies in the Philosophy of Science* (Vol. 1). Minneapolis: University of Minnesota Press, 1956.

MEILAND, J. W. *The nature of intention.* London: Methuen, 1970.

MINSKY, M. (ED.). *Semantic information processing.* Cambridge, Mass.: MIT Press, 1968.

MISCHEL, T. Psychological explanations and their vicissitudes. In W. J. Arnold (Ed.), *Nebraska Symposium on Motivation* (Vol. 25). Lincoln: University of Nebraska Press, 1975.

MONOD, J. *Chance and necessity.* A. Wainhouse, trans. New York: Random House, 1970/1971.

MOORE, J., & NEWELL, A. How can MERLIN understand? In L. W. Gregg (Ed.), *Knowledge and cognition.* Baltimore, Md.: Lawrence Erlbaum, 1974.

NAGEL, T. Physicalism. *Philosophical Review,* 1965, *74*.

NELSON, R. J. Behaviorism is false. *Journal of Philosophy,* 1969, *66*.

NEURATH, O. ET AL. (EDS.). *International encyclopedia of unified science* (Vols. 1–2). Chicago: University of Chicago Press, 1938.

NEWELL, A. Computer science as empirical inquiry: Symbols and search. *Communications of the Association for Computing Machinery,* 1976, *19*.

NEWELL, A., & SIMON, H. A. *Human problem solving.* Englewood Cliffs, N.J.: Prentice-Hall, 1972.

OPPENHEIM, P., & PUTNAM, H. Unity of science as a working hypothesis. In H. Feigl et al. (Eds.), *Minnesota Studies in the Philosophy of Science* (Vol. 2). Minneapolis: University of Minnesota Press, 1958.

PAVLOV, I. P. *Conditioned reflexes.* G. V. Anrep, trans. London: Humphrey Milford, 1927.

PAVLOV, I. P. *Lectures on conditioned reflexes.* W. H. Grantt, trans. New York: International Publishers, 1928.

PENFIELD, W. Speech, perception and the uncommitted cortex. In J. C. Eccles (Ed.), *Brain and conscious experience.* New York: Springer-Verlag, 1965.

PIAGET, J. *Structuralism.* C. Maschler, trans. New York: Basic Books, 1968/1970.

PIAGET, J. The psychogenesis of knowledge and its epistemological significance. In M. Piattelli-Palmarini (Ed.), *Language and learning: The debate between Jean Piaget and Noam Chomsky.* Cambridge, Mass.: Harvard University Press, 1979/1980.

PIATTELLI-PALMARINI, M. (ED.). *Language and learning: The debate between Jean Piaget and Noam Chomsky.* Cambridge, Mass.: Harvard University Press, 1980.

PITCHER, G. *A theory of perception.* Princeton, N.J.: Princeton University Press, 1971.

POLYAK, S. L. *The retina.* Chicago: University of Chicago Press, 1941.

PREMACK, D. *Intelligence in ape and man.* Hillsdale, N.J.: Lawrence Erlbaum, 1976.

PUTNAM, H. Men and machines. In S. Hook (Ed.), *Dimensions of mind.* New York: New York University Press, 1960.

PUTNAM, H. "The innateness hypothesis" and explanatory models in linguistics. *Synthese,* 1967, *17.*

PUTNAM, H. The mental life of some machines. In *Philosophical papers* (Vol. 2). Cambridge, England: Cambridge University Press, 1967/1975. (a)

PUTNAM, H. The nature of mental states. In *Philosophical papers* (Vol. 2). Cambridge, England: Cambridge University Press, 1967/1975. (b)

PUTNAM, H. Logical positivism and the philosophy of mind. In P. Achinstein & S. Barker (Eds.), *The legacy of logical positivism.* Baltimore, Md.: Johns Hopkins University Press, 1969.

PUTNAM, H. The meaning of "meaning." In K. Gunderson (Ed.), *Minnesota Studies in the Philosophy of Science* (Vol. 7). Minneapolis: University of Minnesota Press, 1975.

PUTNAM, H. *Meaning and the moral sciences.* London: Routledge & Kegan Paul, 1978.

PYLYSHYN, Z. W. Complexity and the study of artificial and human intelligence. In M. Ringle (Ed.), *Philosophical perspectives on artificial intelligence.* Atlantic Highlands, N.J.: Humanities Press, 1978.

PYLYSHYN, Z. W. Computation and cognition: Issues in the foundation of cognitive science. *Behavioral and Brain Sciences,* 1980, *3.*

QUINE, W. V. Two dogmas of empiricism. In *From a logical point of view.* Cambridge, Mass.: Harvard University Press, 1953.

QUINE, W. V. *Word and object.* Cambridge, Mass.: MIT Press, 1960.

QUINE, W. V. Linguistics and philosophy. In S. Hook (Ed.), *Language and philosophy.* New York: New York University Press, 1969.

RICOEUR, P. *Hermeneutics and the human sciences.* J. B. Thompson, Ed. and trans. Cambridge, England: Cambridge University Press, 1981.

RORTY, R. Mind–body identity, privacy, and categories. *Review of Metaphysics,* 1965, *19.*

RORTY, R. Incorrigibility as the mark of the mental. *Journal of Philosophy,* 1970, *67.* (a)

RORTY, R. In defense of eliminative materialism. *Review of Metaphysics,* 1970, *24.* (b)

RORTY, R. *Philosophy and the mirror of nature.* Princeton, N.J.: Princeton University Press, 1979.

ROSCH, E. Natural categories. *Cognitive Psychology,* 1973, *4.*

RYLE, G. *The concept of mind.* London: Hutchinson, 1949.

SALMON, W. Statistical explanation. In *Statistical explanation and statistical relevance.* Pittsburgh: University of Pittsburgh Press, 1970.

SAUSSURE, F. DE. *Course in general linguistics.* C. Bally, A. Sechehaye, & A. Riedlinger, Eds.; W. Baskin, trans. New York: McGraw-Hill, 1916/1966.

SEARLE, J. R. Minds, brains, and programs. *Behavioral and Brain Sciences,* 1980, *3.*

SEGALL, M. E. (ED.). *The influence of culture on visual perception.* Indianapolis, Ind.: Bobbs-Merrill, 1966.

SELLARS, W. Philosophy and the scientific image of man. In *Science, perception, and reality.* London: Routledge & Kegan Paul, 1963.

SHAFFER, J. *Philosophy of mind.* Englewood Cliffs, N.J.: Prentice-Hall, 1968.

SHANNON, C. E. A mathematical theory of communication. *Bell System Technical Journal,* 1948, *27.*

SHANNON, C. E., & WEAVER W. *Mathematical theory of communication.* Urbana: University of Illinois Press, 1949.

SIBLEY, F. N. Analysing seeing (1). In F. N. Sibley (Ed.), *Perception: A philosophical symposium.* London: Methuen, 1971.

SKINNER, B. F. *The behavior of organisms.* New York: Appleton-Century-Crofts, 1938.

SKINNER, B. F. *Science and human behavior.* New York: Macmillan, 1953.

SKINNER, B. F. *Verbal behavior.* New York: Appleton-Century-Crofts, 1957.

SKINNER, B. F. Behaviorism at fifty. In T. W. Wann (Ed.), *Behaviorism and phenomenology.* Chicago: University of Chicago Press, 1964.

SKINNER, B. F. *About behaviorism.* New York: Knopf, 1974.

SMART, J.J.C. Sensations and brain processes (rev.). In V. C. Chappell (Ed.), *The philosophy of mind.* Englewood Cliffs, N.J.: Prentice-Hall, 1959/1962.

SMART, J.J.C. *Philosophy and scientific realism.* London: Routledge & Kegan Paul, 1963.

SMITH E. E., & MEDIN, D. L. *Categories and concepts.* Cambridge, Mass.: Harvard University Press, 1981.

SPENCE, K. W. *Behavior theory and conditioning.* New Haven, Conn.: Yale University Press, 1956.

SPERRY, R. W. A modified concept of consciousness. *Psychological Review,* 1969, *76.*

STEBBINS, G. L. The evolutionary significance of biological templates. In A. D. Breck & W. Yourgrau (Eds.), *Biology, history, and natural philosophy.* New York: Plenum, 1972.

STEGMÜLLER, W. The problem of causality. In *Collected papers on epistemology, philosophy of science and history of philosophy* (Vol. 2). B. Martini & W. Wohlhueter, trans. Dordrecht, Holland: Reidel, 1977.

STEVENS, S. S. On the psychological law. *Psychological Review,* 1957, *64*.

STICH, S. P. Empiricism, innatism, and linguistic universals. *Philosophical Studies,* 1978, *33*.

STRAWSON, P. F. *Individuals.* London: Methuen, 1959.

TAYLOR, C. *The explanation of behavior.* London: Routledge & Kegan Paul, 1964.

TERRACE, H. S. Is problem-solving language? In T. S. Sebeok & J. Umiker-Sebeok (Eds.), *Speaking of apes.* New York: Plenum, 1980.

THORNDIKE, E. L. *Selected writings from a connectionist's psychology.* New York: Appleton-Century-Crofts, 1949.

TINBERGEN, N. *The study of instinct.* London: Oxford University Press, 1951/1959.

TOLMAN, E. C. *Behavior and psychological man.* Berkeley: University of California Press, 1958.

TOLMAN, E. C., RITCHIE, B. F., & KALISH, D. Studies in spatial learning: I, Orientation and the shortcut. *Journal of Experimental Psychology,* 1946, *36*.

TURING, A. M. Computing machinery and intelligence. *Mind,* 1950, *59*.

VALZELLI, L. *Psychopharmacology.* New York: Spectrum, 1973.

VENDLER, Z. *Res cogitans.* Ithaca, N.Y.: Cornell University Press, 1972.

VOLOŠINOV, V. N. *Marxism and the philosophy of language.* L. Matejka & I. B. Titunik, trans. New York: Seminar Press, 1973.

VYGOTSKY, L. S. *Thought and language.* E. Hanfmann & G. Vakar, trans. Cambridge, Mass.: MIT Press, 1934/1962.

VYGOTSKY, L. S. *Mind in society.* M. Cole et al., Eds.; A. R. Luria et al., trans. Cambridge, Mass.: Harvard University Press, 1978.

WANN, T. W. (ED.). *Behaviorism and phenomenology.* Chicago: University of Chicago Press, 1964.

WATSON, J. B. Psychology as the behaviorist views it. In W. Dennis (Ed.), *Readings in the history of psychology.* New York: Appleton-Century-Crofts, 1913/1963.

WATSON, J. B. *Behaviorism.* London: Kegan Paul, Trench and Trubner, 1925.

WATSON, J. D. *Molecular biology of the gene* (2nd ed.). Menlo Park, Calif.: W. A. Benjamin, 1970.

WIENER, N. *The human use of human beings.* Boston: Houghton Mifflin, 1950/1954.

WINOGRAD, T. *Understanding natural language.* New York: Academic Press, 1972/1976.

WITTGENSTEIN, L. *Philosophical investigations.* G.E.M. Anscombe, trans. New York: Macmillan, 1953/1963.

For Further Reading

The references give rather too long a list of readings for a convenient entry into the literature, a difficulty the following suggestions may correct. Of the relevant anthologies, these are particularly useful:

BLOCK, N. (ED.). *Readings in philosophy of psychology* (2 vols.). Cambridge, Mass.: Harvard University Press, 1980–1981.

BLOCK, N. *Imagery*. Cambridge, Mass.: MIT Press, 1981.

CHAPPELL, V. C. (ED.). *Philosophy of mind* (Rev. ed.). (Englewood Cliffs, N.J.: Prentice-Hall, 1962.

HAUGELAND, J. (ED.). *Mind design*. Montgomery, Vt.: Bradford Books, 1981.

Excellent collections that are not merely anthologies of established papers include:

RINGLE, M. (ED.). *Philosophical perspectives of artificial intelligence*. Atlantic Highlands, N.J.: Humanities Press, 1978.

SAVAGE, C. W. (ED.). *Minnesota Studies in the Philosophy of Science* (Vol. 9, *Perception and Cognition; Issues in the Foundations of Psychology)*. Minneapolis: University of Minnesota Press, 1978.

The single most useful periodical is the quarterly *The Behavioral and Brain Sciences*.

Among the more recent books of note not included in the References and not featured in the text itself are the following:

CHURCHLAND, P. M. *Scientific realism and the plasticity of mind.* Cambridge, England: Cambridge University Press, 1979.

DRETSKE, F. I. *Knowledge and the flow of information.* Cambridge, Mass.: MIT Press, 1981.

FODOR, J. A. *Representations.* Cambridge, Mass.: MIT Press, 1981.

KOSSLYN, S. M. *Image and mind.* Cambridge, Mass.: Harvard University Press, 1980.

Index